Comments on other *Amazing Stories* ...wers

"*Tightly written volumes filled with k , wit and humour about famous and infamous Canadians.*"
Eric Shackleton, *The Globe and Mail*

"*The heightened sense of drama and intrigue, combined with a good dose of human interest is what sets* Amazing Stories *apart.*"
Pamela Klaffke, *Calgary Herald*

"*This is popular history as it should be... For this price, buy two and give one to a friend.*"
Terry Cook, a reader from Ottawa, on **Rebel Women**

"*Glasner creates the moment of the explosion itself in graphic detail...she builds detail upon gruesome detail to create a convincingly authentic picture.*"
Peggy McKinnon, *The Sunday Herald*, on **The Halifax Explosion**

"*It was wonderful...I found I could not put it down.*

M   *II*

"*A   ng*

I   ;

GREAT DEFENCEMEN

AMAZING STORIES®

GREAT DEFENCEMEN

Stars of Hockey's Golden Age

HOCKEY

by Jim Barber

PUBLISHED BY ALTITUDE PUBLISHING CANADA LTD.
1500 Railway Avenue, Canmore, Alberta T1W 1P6
www.altitudepublishing.com
www.amazingstories.ca
1-800-957-6888

Extreme care has been taken to ensure that all information presented in
this book is accurate and up to date. Neither the author nor the
publisher can be held responsible for any errors.

Publisher	Stephen Hutchings
Associate Publisher	Kara Turner
Editors	Frances Purslow and Ros Penty
Cover and layout	Bryan Pezzi

We acknowledge the financial support of the Government
of Canada through the Book Publishing Industry Development
Program (BPIDP) for our publishing activities.

Altitude GreenTree Program 🌲
Altitude Publishing will plant twice as many trees as were used
in the manufacturing of this product.

Library and Archives Canada Cataloguing in Publication

Barber, Jim (Jim Christopher Matthew)
Great defencemen / Jim Barber.

(Amazing stories)
Includes bibliographical references.
ISBN 1-55439-083-4

1. Hockey players--Biography. 2. National Hockey League--Biography.
3. Hockey--Defense. I. Title. II. Series: Amazing stories (Canmore, Alta.)

GV848.5.A1B266 2006   796.962'092'2   C2005-906891-4

Printed and bound in Canada by Friesens
2 4 6 8 9 7 5 3 1

To the players who raised the level of defensive play
to that of an athletic art form.

Contents

Prologue

The Detroit Red Wings were pressing, hoping to steal the lead from the New York Rangers. It was a mid-season contest, but for the Wings, who were looking to challenge the Toronto Maple Leafs' dominance of the National Hockey League (NHL), every point, every goal counted.

The Rangers were just trying to not get blown out by the powerful Wings.

The puck, suddenly lobbed deep into New York territory, slid into the corner, not far from goaltender Chuck Rayner.

There was a foot race between 22-year-old rookie Ranger rearguard Allan Stanley, the pride of Timmins, Ontario, and the streaking James Enio.

Enio was not a regular member of the Red Wings' roster, but sure wanted to be. If he could make an impact early in the game, through a big hit, a fight, or a goal, he might gain the favour of manager Jack Adams, and a permanent spot on the roster.

With a loud clatter of stick and skates, Stanley — all 6'1", 175 pounds of him — collided in the corner with Enio, who was just a couple of inches shorter.

Both players lost their balance in the two-player pile-up, as the crowd roared its appreciation of the thunderous collision.

Somehow, Stanley landed on top of Enio, who was lying on his back. Stanley's arms were extended and pressing against the winged-wheel crest on the Red Wing jersey beneath him. In effect, Enio was being held in place.

Suddenly, Stanley, who was watching to see where the play had gone, felt a short sharp clinching pain in one of his forearms. He looked down to see an enraged Enio looking more like a pitbull than a man, with his teeth dug into his arm.

The absurdity of the situation momentarily dulled the pain.

And that's how one of the greatest defencemen of the Original Six Era was introduced to the grace, class, and elegance of the NHL.

Introduction

In the formative days of professional hockey, solid defence-men were the unsung heroes of the game. For much of the early decades of hockey, the perfect defenceman was a silent sentinel, whose only job was to check oncoming forwards and prevent them from getting a shot on net.

Defencemen were not expected to score points. If they did, it was a bonus, and meant they had a decent outlet pass. If they scored an actual goal, it was unusual, and meant they were either very lucky or very bold.

Size was important, but not as critical as a defenceman's ability to stay solid on his feet and to deliver a hard body-check that at the very least impeded an opponent's forward progress, or, better yet, knocked him on his hind quarters. A slightly vicious streak was a benefit as well, as long as it didn't lead to too many penalties.

If a defenceman's name made the papers, it was usu-ally for one of three reasons: he allowed an enemy forward by him, he failed to clear the puck out of his own zone, or he took a dumb penalty that cost a goal or a game. If he gener-ated no headlines, or barroom chatter, he was doing his job.

The seven athletes profiled in this book are not these sorts of defencemen. These blueliners generated headlines, not for the things they screwed up, but for the way they took the traditional role of the defenceman and broadened its scope.

Through incredible versatility, longevity, brilliant puck-handling, exceptional skating, a cannonading shot, or deft passing, these men changed the way defencemen played the game, and the nature of hockey itself.

They were colourful, controversial, and crafty. They scored, they fought, they teased, they tortured. These exceptional seven were the cream of the crop as far as blueliners go in the Golden Age of the NHL. They paved the way for the likes of Bobby Orr, Larry Robinson, Brad Park, Paul Coffey, and Chris Pronger, most of whom embody the same mixture of talent, toughness, skill, and savvy.

Clancy, Clapper, Harvey, Horton, Shore, Stanley, and Johnson were the most amazing defencemen of hockey's Golden Era.

Chapter 1
Francis "King" Clancy: The King of Hockey

rancis "King" Clancy is so remembered as a Toronto Maple Leaf, that many hockey fans forget he first became a star in the National Hockey League with his hometown Ottawa Senators.

Blessed with speed and balance, he was a whirlwind on blades, and a rarity in the NHL of the early 1920s — he was a defenceman who could carry the puck up the ice with the same pluck, poise, and potency as a forward.

But one critical game in particular propelled Clancy from the status of hometown boy made good, to hockey legend. That night in 1923, he played every single position on the team, to help the Ottawa Senators win the Stanley Cup.

The Senators had won the NHL title with a 14-9-1

record, which earned them the right to challenge the best from the west for hockey supremacy.

Since 1913, the most famous trophy in hockey history was awarded to the team that won a series between the champions of the National Hockey Association (forerunner of the National Hockey League) and the champions of the Pacific Coast Hockey Association (PCHA).

Over the years, the PCHA suffered a number of up and downs, including the recent addition of a rival league — the Western Canadian Hockey League (WCHL). So in 1923, for the first time, the winner of the Stanley Cup would have to defeat two rival claimants to have their names inscribed on the big silver bowl. The winner of the series between the NHL and the PCHA would face the champions of the WCHL for the Stanley Cup.

The games would all be played in Vancouver. After defeating the home team, the Senators now faced the Edmonton Eskimos in the best-two-of-three series.

In a hard-fought opening contest, the Senators managed to squeak through with a 2-1 win. In the second game of the series, 9,000 fans in Vancouver witnessed an incredible bit of history.

Clancy was a substitute, as, in those days, players routinely played almost every minute of every game.

In the first period, regular defencemen Eddie Gerard and Buck Boucher both suffered minor injuries at different points of the game, and Clancy filled in, admirably, both times. He took many more bodychecks than he handed out, but he never stayed down for long — the tenacity inherited from his father (Thomas "King" Clancy, a star athlete in his own right) was now paying dividends.

Soon enough, Clancy found himself back on the bench. In the second period, an Edmonton player managed to get hold of Clancy's teammate, Frank Nighbor, for a fair but hard check, which temporarily knocked the wind out of the man considered to be the greatest centre of his era. As a doubled-over, gasping Nighbor returned slowly to the bench, coach Tommy Gorman ordered Clancy onto the ice again. A few in the crowd that night must have been wondering who this little powerhouse was. They could hear his high-pitched voice cackling encouragement from the bench for most of the game, and now they watched him do yeoman's work every time his skates hit the ice.

Later, star left winger Cy Denneny caught an errant stick and was cut. Bleeding, he came off the ice for repairs, and Clancy got the nod again. Soon thereafter, Punch Broadbent, who had spent every minute on the ice chasing Eskimos around, skated to the bench, haggard and exhausted. Out Clancy went, this time at right wing.

Five positions in one game was an incredible feat, and would remain an incredible hockey story to this day. But the truly amazing part of this story came later. Senators' star netminder Clint Benedict was given a two-minute penalty for slashing an Edmonton player who glided a little too close to him. In those days, goaltenders had to serve their own penalties. As well, players had to serve the entire two-minute sentence, no matter how many goals the other team scored.

The Senators were in a real pickle: their goalie was in the penalty box. And they were trying to hold onto a 1-0 lead against a team that was fighting for its very survival. They decided to put their diminutive substitute player in goal. Clancy was undaunted. He grabbed Benedict's goal stick and set up shop between the pipes.

In front of him, the rest of the Senators did everything humanly possible to prevent the Eskimos from getting a scoring chance. Blanketed by Ottawa's stifling defensive formation, Edmonton resorted to firing long-distance volleys, hoping one might skip past Clancy. When the penalty had nearly expired, the puck again was fired deep into the Ottawa zone. Seeing an opening, Clancy raced over, grabbed the puck, and proceeded to skate up the ice with it. Juggling the puck as best as he could with Benedict's cumbersome stick, Clancy actually managed to skate all the way into the Edmonton zone, and get a shot on Eskimos' goalie Hal Winkler, to the delight of the crowd. The Senators would hold on to win the game 1-0 and the Stanley Cup.

It not only took talent to perform such a feat, it also took a great deal of courage and guile. King Clancy had these in spades, along with healthy doses of charm, a bit of Irish luck, and an unmatched work ethic.

Francis Clancy grew up in the shadow of his father, Thomas "King" Clancy, a legend in the local sporting community. Tom also literally cast a shadow over his son, standing six feet tall, and weighing in at a solid 200 pounds.

Francis was neither a natural athlete, nor did he measure up to his father's physical stature. He did, however, inherit Tom Clancy's drive to succeed and his aggressive desire to overcome any and all obstacles.

Around Ottawa, Francis's pluck and tenacity gained him the epithet "King" also.

At age 16, after a couple of seasons in the local high school and amateur hockey leagues, and weighing only 130 pounds, the younger Clancy convinced the coach of a senior level team sponsored by St. Brigid's Athletic Club in Ottawa to allow him on the roster.

Although he made the team, he spent most of the season planted on the bench. The coach wasn't convinced the diminutive Clancy could stand up to the pounding. In his second year with the team, he played eight games, thanks to one of the first-string blueliners showing up inebriated one day. Clancy took his spot, and soon found himself logging more and more ice time, while drawing attention and accolades.

In 1920–1921, Clancy scored six goals in 11 games, and caught the eye of Tommy Gorman, the manager of the Ottawa Senators — the city's top team and member of the four-year-old National Hockey League.

The following summer, Gorman ran into Tom Clancy

and said he'd like to have a chat with his 18-year-old son. Both Clancys thought that Gorman, who also owned the racetrack in town, wanted to speak with Francis about a summer job mucking out stables.

Instead, Gorman said he wanted Francis to play for the Senators.

"Right then I almost dropped dead. I had no idea I was good enough to play hockey for the Ottawa Senators," the younger Clancy said years later.

He was offered a contract for $800, and would practise with the team, as well as act as emergency substitute in games.

It was a dream come true for a home-grown player. The Senators boasted some of the most talented and exciting players in the game. Clancy was in awe.

"I was as green as grass and got the shakes just thinking about skating on the same ice surface with men who were famous from one end of the country to the other for their hockey exploits," he said.

The same courage and guile that he possessed as a young man carried over into his playing days, sometimes with potentially dangerous consequences. He was known for starting a lot of fights, but not finishing too many, often picking fights with much bigger, stronger opponents.

On one of the rare occasions when he saw real game action in his rookie season with the Senators, he found himself on the ice against the Montreal Canadiens. The 1921–1922 version of the Canadiens was tough, featuring the likes of Sprague Cleghorn and Bert "Pig Iron" Corbeau. Corbeau didn't earn his nickname from fancy pirouettes or sparkling plays. He was a strong, aggressive defenceman who could bodycheck an unsuspecting opponent into the middle of next week, as well as contribute a respectable amount of offence for a blueliner.

Deciding that the youngster from Ottawa hadn't been properly introduced to top-flight professional hockey, Corbeau proceeded to cross-check Clancy to the back of the neck and into the chicken wire at the end of the rink. As Clancy slid to the ground, Corbeau landed on him — knees first.

Irish blood boiling, Clancy rose quickly and smashed his stick over Corbeau's sizeable back.

"He didn't even flinch. I don't think he even noticed!" Clancy said.

As both players were being ushered to the penalty box, Clancy tripped Corbeau just as he was stepping off the ice. The big man got up, and glared at his uppity young adversary. He predicted that if Clancy didn't change his behaviour and show due respect to his elders, he wouldn't last two weeks in the league.

Clancy was still playing 16 years later.

The following season — the year he played all positions in the finals — Clancy won his first Stanley Cup

The Senators made the playoffs in 1924 and 1926, but didn't make it back to the Stanley Cup finals again until 1927, the first year that the Cup would be contended strictly by NHL teams (the WCHL and PCHA having folded the previous year.)

The Senators finished first in the NHL standings in 1926–1927, dumping the Canadiens in the semi-finals before meeting the Boston Bruins in the finals. The teams tied 0-0 in the first game, while Ottawa took the second game 3-1. The teams tied the next game, and Ottawa took the series and the Cup in the deciding contest. It would be the last time the team would be a factor in Stanley Cup competition.

While the team struggled, Clancy did not, and kept adding colourful stories to his already burgeoning legend.

In the late 1920s, former Montreal tough guy Sprague Cleghorn, who was known for his explosive temper, was playing out his final days as a defenceman with Boston. In one memorable game near the end of his career, a number of Ottawa players were rushing up the ice with the puck, when the wily Cleghorn stole the disc and began plodding up the ice in the direction of Senators' netminder Alex Connell. Clancy, who had been part of the rush, was able to scoot back to within earshot of Cleghorn. As he pulled in behind Cleghorn, he called for the puck, as if he were a teammate joining the play. Cleghorn laid a perfect pass onto the stick of the speedy Clancy, who was able to clear the puck out of danger.

Cleghorn's anger at having a potential scoring play messed up was compounded by the humiliation of having fallen for such an amateurish, schoolboy ruse.

After the game ended, Clancy was about to walk through

the door into the Senators' dressing room, when a bellow from behind stopped him in his tracks. With no chance to defend himself, a Cleghorn fist to the nose floored Clancy. As Clancy dropped to the ground, bleeding badly from both nostrils, Cleghorn simply walked away into his team's dressing room.

Whether Clancy ever tried to pull that stunt again on Cleghorn is not known, but there are certainly no more stories of him getting smacked by the big bruiser.

As the 1920s drew to a close, the Senators' roster began a wholesale change. As players retired, the team dropped in the standings. Team owners were swimming in red ink and they needed to shed good players for as much cash as they could get in return. (In those days, teams could "trade" a player for cash.)

Clancy was coveted by a number of teams, but his most persistent suitor was Maple Leafs owner Conn Smythe.

The Senators were asking $35,000 in cash, plus some players. Smythe accepted that the price was probably as good as it was going to get, but he didn't have all the money.

He approached some business associates and the directors of the team and raised $25,000. That was still well short of the asking price. One day, Smythe decided to enter a horse he owned, called Rare Jewel, in the Coronation Stakes — a prestigious race with a substantial purse.

Rare Jewel was rare all right; she had never yet managed to find the winner's circle. She was listed at odds of 107-1, but Smythe was feeling lucky.

Rare Jewel won that day — the only race she would ever win. Smythe was able to pick up more than $12,000 from wagering plus the winner's purse of nearly $3,600. He added his race-track winnings to the $25,000 and threw in a couple of fringe players and in return, he got the dynamic, exciting, energetic, talented player that he felt his Leafs needed.

By the time the team got Clancy, they had assembled a blueline corps that featured future Hall of Famers Clarence "Hap" Day and Red Horner. Up front, the Leafs were blessed with the so-called Kid Line of Joe Primeau, Charlie Conacher, and Harvey "Busher" Jackson. Clancy added enthusiasm and infectious, optimistic energy to the mix, along with incredible talent.

The crowds at the Mutual Street Arena in Toronto were soon too large for that venue. Smythe realized that the Leafs needed a new arena to become profitable. Maple Leaf Gardens was a hockey palace when it was completed in time for the start of the 1931–1932 NHL season — a palace fit for a King.

For much of his career, Clancy was considered to be among the top defencemen in the entire league. The one fellow who was always rated ahead of him, and even Clancy would accede to that, was Boston's Eddie Shore. Unlike Clancy, Shore was already a hardened veteran of the professional hockey wars when he came to the NHL in 1924. Hated in every building in the NHL except for the Boston Garden where he was revered like an Olympian god, Shore was mean, tough, and phenomenally talented.

Clancy loved to get under Shore's skin. Shore would occasionally retaliate, but must have had a grudging respect for the plucky little loudmouth, because he let him live. Not long after Clancy joined the Leafs, the team was playing Shore and the Bruins. After a rush up the ice, Shore found himself knocked to his knees in the Toronto zone, not far from goaltender Lorne Chabot. Clancy was nearby, and for no reason other than to stir up some mischief, he popped Shore with a hard uppercut. Shore was incensed but didn't chase after him; instead he got up and challenged Clancy to try the same thing again. With a straight face, Clancy said he'd be happy to oblige, if Shore would get back on his knees. Then he turned and skated away.

Shore and Clancy were the two of the key performers in another on-ice drama that did not have such a humorous tone.

In a game played in mid-December 1933 in the Boston Garden, Clancy tripped Shore as he was carrying the puck. This humiliation provoked Shore into a blind rage. He sought out the first player he could find wearing a blue and white sweater, and knocked the unsuspecting man ass over tea kettle. A completely innocent Ace Bailey landed on his head, cracking his skull. Shore simply skated away with a satisfied smile. Bailey nearly died.

Clancy witnessed it all first hand and he contends that although Shore liked to hit hard, he did not deliberately plot to end a fellow player's career. "Shore wasn't a vicious player, although he knew he was playing a rough game. He wasn't out there to maim anybody but simply to make his living," Clancy said.

Although Clancy was jovial by nature, he was also highly competitive, and not above a little malicious revenge himself.

One night, toward the end of the 1933–1934 season, the Leafs were playing the New York Rangers. It was a typical game between the two teams. Rough but not overly nasty, hard checking, lots of action, and a close score.

As King Clancy crossed centre ice at one point in the game he collided hard with the Rangers' Art Somers, a man of similar stature. The play looked innocent enough, but Clancy retreated to the bench with blood pouring from his mouth and four teeth missing. Clancy claimed that Somers turned so that the butt end of his stick would deliberately hit him in the mouth. Although Clancy had been the brunt of many a heinous attack, and suffered innumerable injuries, he rarely waited long to even the score.

In the 1930s, having only a 48-game season, NHL players had nearly six months off between seasons. Before the season ended, Clancy decided how he could wreak his revenge on Somers and get away with it. He kept the memory of this indignity alive through the long, hot summer.

Before the start of the next season, Clancy tore open a pair of elbow pads and removed some of the felt padding. Then he cracked open some shotgun shells, and filled the pads with lead pellets, leaving enough padding in them to resemble ordinary elbow pads.

King Clancy

Clancy waited for the first game of the 1934–1935 season between the Rangers and Leafs before putting on the pads. At the first opportunity, Clancy saw Somers skating up the ice and decided the time was ripe for a little payback. Somers had his head down, probably watching the play develop, or waiting for a pass, Clancy nailed him with the now potently metallic elbow, knocking Somers senseless. His jaw was broken in 14 places.

Somers needed surgery to repair the damage, and complications set in. Somers was on the shelf for much of that season, seeing action in only seven games for the Rangers after a short rehabilitation stint with the Windsor Bulldogs of the International Hockey League.

Clancy was regarded as one of the top blueliners of the 1930s, and was a perennial All-Star. But other than their triumph in winning the Stanley Cup in 1932, that would be Toronto's only championship title while Clancy was a player. However, that doesn't mean things weren't still exciting and interesting when he was around Maple Leaf Gardens.

Early in the second game of a total-goals two-game preliminary-round playoff series with the Bruins in 1936, Charlie Conacher elbowed a member of the Bruins and got away with it. Eddie Shore was already steamed about the non-call from the referee, when he himself was subsequently upended by Clancy. Again, no call.

When Shore confronted the referee, Clancy stuck with him, egging him on, saying that he was robbed, that the referee was putting one over on him. Shore lost his cool, and fired the puck at the referee. It missed, but the ref gave Shore a two-minute penalty. Now completely incensed, Shore fired another puck up into the crowd at Maple Leaf Gardens, incurring a 10-minute misconduct, to the delight of a now chortling Clancy.

The Leafs were down 4-0 when Shore went into the penalty box, but were tied 4-4 when he returned to the ice. Emboldened, the Maple Leafs scored four more times, winning the game 8-4.

At the end of the 1936–1937 season, Clancy decided the wear and tear on his body was too much, so he retired. He wasn't having as much fun on the ice, and the aches and pains that had developed from too many years of being a small player running into bigger opponents had prematurely worn him out. He was never the same player.

He did return to play in the Howie Morenz tribute game later in 1937, an exhibition contest that saw a team of NHL All-Stars take on the Montreal Canadiens, with the proceeds from the game going to help Morenz's widow and children.

Clancy would collect a paycheque from the sport of hockey for the rest of his life. He coached the Montreal Maroons for a season and then refereed in the NHL for 11 seasons. He coached the Maple Leafs for parts of three seasons in the mid-1950s, and filled in for Punch Imlach in the 1960s. When Harold Ballard took over the team, Clancy became a vice-president in title, but for the most part, was paid to be a goodwill ambassador for the team in the community.

He was beloved by later generations of players and the media, and he always had a joke or a semi-truthful hockey tale to tell.

It was a testament to his enduring popularity that when he died in November 1986, thousands of fans lined up for an opportunity to pay their respects to a man who loved the game, and played with an infectious passion, a wry smirk, a gleam in his eye, and an indefatigable zest for life.

Chapter 2
Eddie Shore: The Biggest, Baddest Bruin

rt Ross, coach/manager for the Boston Bruins, didn't believe in reputations. He believed in cold, hard, empirical facts.

In one training camp scrimmage during the early 1920s, he was watching Eddie Shore, a kid from the Prairies who was known in the amateur and minor pro leagues for being both tough and talented. But this was the NHL — the fastest, most punishing league in the world. A yokel from small-town Saskatchewan with a chip on his shoulder at his first big league training camp would be no match for a grizzled veteran of the NHL wars.

Or so Ross thought.

Veteran player Billy Coutu also knew a little about

Shore's reputation and certainly didn't like the cockiness with which he carried himself around the ice. Coutu decided to teach Shore a lesson and unnerve the brash rookie, while Ross sat back and enjoyed the show.

And what a show it was.

Coutu was a pugnacious player who was nearing the end of a pretty good career, most of which was spent in Montreal. He never backed down from any challenger and seemed to enjoy the physical punishment he could inflict.

In one scrimmage Coutu and Shore came together, neither man giving way, as one slammed his body into the other. Soon, the bodychecks escalated to punches. Coutu popped Shore, breaking a couple of teeth. Shore responded with a piston-like shot of his own.

Coutu didn't like that Shore was so keen to retaliate, and after this brief skirmish, he decided to change tactics.

Later in the scrimmage, he grabbed the puck, and accelerated straight for Shore. It soon became clear to everyone watching that Coutu wasn't trying to score a goal: he was settling a score.

Shore may have been a little green as far as the NHL was concerned, but he was no dummy. He knew what Coutu had in mind. A more nervous or deferential player in his position would probably have tried to move out of the way, or offer only a half-hearted attempt to stop Coutu, but not Eddie Shore.

Coutu had gained a full head of steam as he hurtled

down the ice. Shore stood his ground, fearlessly staring into eyes of the machine bearing down on him. He had developed a technique of always keeping his knees bent legs wide apart, which allowed for greater balance. It also allowed him to dig them more firmly into the ice. There was a huge collective gasp as the irresistible force met the immovable object.

After the cataclysmic collision, Shore was still standing, bloodied, but not broken. Coutu was lying on the ice, looking up at Shore, his face red with anger and embarrassment.

Shore had made his point, and Ross realized he had the new cornerstone of his young Boston Bruins franchise.

As impressive as this story is, it isn't over yet. Shore's left ear was dangling in a bloody mess on the side of his head after the hit. The doctor on hand told Shore he was going to lose the ear.

Shore disagreed. Other doctors were summoned until one agreed to repair the ear — to Shore's specifications.

"It was not a simple procedure, and with the aid of a mirror, Eddie instructed the physician just how he wanted the job done, almost like a customer telling the barber how to part his hair," penned author Stan Fischler.

Like many other great stories of the game of hockey, the legend of Eddie Shore began on the blustery, expansive Canadian Prairies.

Born in Fort Qu'Appelle, Saskatchewan, in 1902, Eddie and his family moved to nearby Cupar when he was five.

Shore was independent even as a youngster, often getting into trouble at school for disagreeing with his teachers. He was expected to help out on the family farm, and developed great strength and flexibility through his extensive chores, which included breaking wild horses and tending cattle.

When he was nine years old, Shore suffered his first of many broken noses. But it didn't come from a high stick, errant elbow, or face-first encounter with rink boards; it came from a feisty young pony. Shore was trying to apply horseshoes when the animal suddenly reared up catching the youngster flush in the face. Although bleeding and in great pain, Shore finished his chore before going to the house for facial repairs.

Not long after the horse incident, Eddie's older brother, Aubrey, was trying out for one of the local hockey teams, and he berated his little brother for his lack of skating ability. Stubborn pride rose in the heart and mind of Eddie, and he was determined that not only would he learn how to skate, but that he would make the same Cupar school team. In temperatures plummeting to –40 degrees Celsius (–40 degrees Fahrenheit), Eddie worked at every facet of the game. He made that school team, and spent the better part of the next six decades deeply immersed in the game of hockey.

His natural talent and rough-and-tumble personality shone through. Shore soon became a top player in his town, and rose quickly through the hockey ranks, eventually joining the Melville Millionaires, one of the best teams in the Saskatchewan Senior Hockey League at the time.

Tough, brash centre Eddie Shore was their star attraction during the 1923–1924 season. But he was volatile and often garnered several penalties during a game.

Before an important game against Winnipeg, Shore's coach was worried that they would lose if they had to play too much of it short-handed. He implored his feisty young hellion to keep his cool, no matter the cost. For the benefit of his team, Shore agreed, and after a while, the players on the Winnipeg team deduced that the reputedly quarrelsome Shore was actually pretty passive.

Shore endured slashes, cross checks, butt ends, body-checks, elbows to the noggin, and shots to the gut; anywhere the opposing players could find a piece of Eddie Shore, they took their best shot.

And there was no retaliation. Shore played 50 minutes that game. He would have probably gone the entire hour, but the third time he was knocked out, it was decided that his prone form should be taken to the dressing room.

The manager of the team from Saskatoon in the same senior league as Melville happened to be at the game. What he saw of Shore didn't impress him much. This young fellow allowed himself to take a pasting without so much as a peep of protest.

So, the next time the two teams met, the Saskatoon coach told his players they could have their way with this cowardly young upstart.

A player by the name of Bill Cook decided to give Shore a try. Early in the game, Cook had the young forward all lined up and was ready to plaster him against the boards. Shore saw it coming, absorbed the hit, and then fired back with such ferocity that Cook slid halfway across the rink on his backside. Cook's look of astonishment was only surpassed by the look of cool rage on Shore's visage. He was not under any sort of pacifistic orders from his coach on this night.

By the time Shore signed his first professional contract in 1924 with the Regina Caps of the Western Canadian Hockey League, he had converted to playing defence. Two years later, when Lester Patrick folded the western league, Shore was part of a package of players purchased by the two-year-old Boston NHL franchise.

Fans of the Bruins soon fell in love with his brash, take-no-prisoners style, as well as his obvious talent. The Bruins had been fishing around for an identity, something to set them apart from the other teams. From the moment Shore laid out his first opponent with a ferocious bodycheck, they became the Big Bad Bruins. Shore would come to epitomize the raw brutality and finesse of Bruins hockey — a mantle that would be picked up by the likes of Wayne Cashman, Terry O'Reilly, and Cam Neely in future generations.

Shore scored 12 goals in his rookie NHL season — an amazing total for a defenceman. He was also one of the most penalized players in the league, with 130 minutes. The following season, he led the league with 165 penalty minutes and helped his team to the Stanley Cup finals, where they lost to the New York Rangers.

By the end of his second season, Shore had become the most reviled visiting player in the NHL — and he loved the distinction. He didn't care about being popular with fans and players: he just wanted to help his team win. And that may have been the most infuriating element of Shore's game. The Bruins were not only causing mayhem on the ice, they were winning a lot of games.

In the 1928–1929 campaign, Boston topped the American Division of the NHL with 57 points in 44 games playing out of their new rink, the Boston Garden. The Bruins defeated the Canadiens in three games, two by shutout, before winning the finals against the New York Rangers. Shore and the rest of the Bruin defence allowed only one goal in the two-game, total-goals series, while Eddie led all playoff performers with 28 penalty minutes.

Shore and the Bruins had won their first ever Stanley Cup. It would not be their last under his stormy leadership.

Meanwhile, Shore's belligerence had created many enemies throughout the league. Eddie Shore and the Montreal Maroons had a particularly turbulent relationship, likely due to an incident in 1929.

Shore apparently checked Babe Siebert, after the Maroons' tough customer had fallen down behind his own goal. Whether it was a cheap shot or Shore simply couldn't stop his momentum in time, the Maroons preferred to believe that Shore deliberately tried to hurt Siebert. They reckoned some retribution was in order.

"A long-reaching stick blade tore open his cheek. Another sliced his chin ... [another] Maroon player cut across Shore and deliberately gave him a sickening smash to the mouth, which knocked out several teeth," wrote venerable Montreal sportswriter Elmer Ferguson. After the game, Ferguson approached Shore, expecting to hear some venomous vitriol directed at the Maroons.

"Rough going Eddie," said Ferguson to Shore as the bruised and battered Bruin stood under the piercing jets of a hot shower.

Through bloody lips, Shore answered laconically, "It's all in the game. I'll pay off."

One of the most remarkable stories relating to Shore's early tenure with the Bruins had nothing to do with his on-ice performance, but does reflect his much-publicized tenacity.

On January 2, 1929, Shore had attended a fancy dinner party to celebrate the new year in the posh Boston suburb of Brookline. He arranged to leave in time to meet the rest of the Bruins at the train station, as they were en route to a game in Montreal.

On the way into the heart of the city, his cab got caught in a massive traffic jam due to an accident. By the time Shore arrived at the station, the train had already left.

Shore wasn't going to let a missed train prevent him from getting to the game. No other trains were heading out that night, and a sudden blizzard had cancelled all flights. He telephoned the host of the dinner party, and the wealthy businessman arranged to have his chauffeur pick Shore up at the train station, and drive him all the way to Montreal. Unfortunately, the blizzard had intensified, and the chauffeur was not used to driving in such inhospitable weather. Shore, irritated with the nervous driver, ordered him to pull over. For a boy raised in southern Saskatchewan, this blizzard was nothing to fear. Shore banished the driver to the back seat, took the wheel himself, then proceeded to plow through the blizzard. Legend has it that Shore pressed on for nearly 24 hours straight, arriving in Montreal nearly delirious from sleep deprivation.

He arrived in the afternoon, a few hours before game time. In the hotel, he ran into teammates Cooney Weiland and Dit Clapper. He barked at them to wake him up in half an hour. At the appointed time, they tried to shake him awake, and finally resorted to a bucket of ice water. Barely awake, Shore staggered into the dressing room at the Forum and clumsily pulled on his equipment. He scored the lone goal in a 1-0 triumph over Howie Morenz, Aurel Joliat, George Hainsworth, and the rest of the Montreal Canadiens. Manager Art Ross fined Shore $200 for missing the train.

The season after winning the Stanley Cup, Shore and the Bruins were unstoppable. The 1929–1930 season was only the team's sixth in the NHL, and the beginning of the fourth season of Shore's tenure with the team, yet it proved to be one of the most remarkable regular seasons in the history of the league. In 44 league games, Boston won an incred-

Eddie Shore

ible 38, losing only five and tying one other, for a winning percentage of .875. Shore solidified his status as not only a nasty and bruising defenceman, but a supremely talented one as well, scoring 12 goals and adding 19 assists for a total of 31 points.

Shore continued to be a dominant player in the league. Respect soon replaced blind hatred in the minds of many hockey fans, as his remarkable career and the legend of his toughness grew.

Just as it seemed Shore was beginning to earn the affections of the hockey world, the "Ace Bailey Incident" occurred, forever tainting Shore's reputation.

By all accounts, Irvine "Ace" Bailey was a decent enough chap. No shrinking violet, he earned his share of penalty minutes in the NHL since joining the league with the Toronto St. Patricks, which were shortly thereafter renamed the Maple Leafs. He and Eddie Shore began in the league at the same time, and both had become important players for their respective teams.

On December 12, 1933, the Bruins hosted the Maple Leafs, and the game was soon teetering on the brink of all-out war.

Shore was his usual unpleasant self, and the Maple Leafs' Red Horner — never a slouch in the rambunctious department — was creating a little mayhem in return. However, both teams made it through the first period more or less intact.

There is some debate as to whether Shore simply lost his composure during the game, or whether he was already seeking revenge for some previous slight. In the second period, the Maple Leafs were assessed two consecutive minor penalties, so the Bruins were on a five-on-three power play. Dick

Irvin Sr., the Leafs' coach, did what any smart coach would do in such a situation: he sent out his two best defencemen — Red Horner and Francis "King" Clancy — as well as his most defensive-minded forward, Irvine "Ace" Bailey.

Bailey won the first face-off and managed to carry the puck around the ice, eluding the entire Bruins team, for nearly a minute.

When he won the next face-off, he ragged the puck again, before firing it the length of the ice into the Bruins' end. Shore retrieved the puck and began to race up the ice, trying to capitalize on the waning power play.

He never made it past King Clancy, as the 140-pound defenceman somehow derailed the onrushing Shore, tripping him up, and then stealing the puck as Eddie tried to get his skates under him. This was an embarrassing turn of events for the fiercely proud Bruin stalwart. The lit fuse had now reached the powder keg — an explosion was imminent.

Blind with fury, and a little disoriented from the unceremonious upending, Shore looked around to see where the culprit was. By this time, Ace Bailey had moved back to the blue line to fill in for Clancy, who was up near the Boston goal.

Whether Shore simply wanted to punish the first Maple Leaf player he saw, or he assumed the player with his back to him, huffing and puffing in the defensive position, was the player who had tripped him, Shore mustered all the power his legs could create and charged at Ace Bailey with retribution on his mind.

The crowd was so noisy that Bailey could not hear the crunching of the ice growing louder behind him, and his teammates on the Toronto bench didn't warn him, as their attention, like Bailey's, was focused up the ice.

Shore, knees bent, legs chugging, put his shoulder down into Bailey's midsection; eyewitnesses claim it was near his kidneys. The force of the hit and its location caused Bailey's body to bend backward and then go airborne, feet in the air, head down.

Then came the sound. The crowd, momentarily silent, must have been mesmerized by Bailey's involuntary acrobatics, because when Bailey's head connected with the ice, the sickening sound of the impact could be heard throughout the arena.

As Bailey lay prone on the ice, his head turned awkwardly to the side, knees raised, legs beginning to go into grotesque spasm, Shore simply skated back to his defensive position.

Bailey's skull had been cracked like an egg, but no one knew that at the time. Nor did they realize just how close to death he would come. After tending to his fallen comrade, an enraged Horner confronted Shore, asking him why he so viciously attacked Bailey. It appeared that Shore either didn't know exactly what happened, or didn't care. Horner assumed it was the latter, and responded to Shore's smug smile and silence with the hardest punch he'd ever thrown.

"It was a right uppercut that stiffened the big defence

star like an axed steer," wrote Leaf assistant manager, Frank Selke, years later. "As he fell, with his body rigid and straight as a board, Shore's head struck the ice, splitting open. In an instant, he was circled by a pool of blood about three feet in diameter."

Then the two fallen soldiers were carried off the ice on stretchers by their respective teammates.

In many eyes, Shore had crossed a line. His action was seen by some as a deliberate attempt to injure. Leaf owner, Conn Smythe, sure felt this way. With the backing of some of his fellow league owners, Smythe lobbied for Shore to be suspended for the rest of the season.

For his part, Shore claims there was nothing about his actions for him to feel badly about. "I had been tripped and struck my head. I didn't realize I had hit Bailey. Another thing I couldn't recall was Red Horner's encounter with me. One thing I can say for sure is that I had no malice toward Ace Bailey. Whatever injury I caused him was purely accidental."

League officials felt that Shore's hit, while hard, was not intended to injure Bailey or any other Maple Leaf player. Shore was tagged with a 16-game suspension, and spent the time recuperating in the Caribbean, on a trip paid for by the Bruins. Bailey never played hockey again.

But Bailey himself, once he recovered, was willing to forgive and forget, even if many others weren't. He minimized the incident by claiming that Shore didn't see him, and that the hit was just part of the game.

A few weeks after the Shore hit on Bailey, the league held its first All-Star game. It featured the Toronto Maple Leafs facing off against the best in the rest of the league. Eddie Shore was on that team. The proceeds from the game ($25,000) were given to Bailey and his family.

One of the most dramatic moments in the history of the NHL occurred when it was Shore's turn to be introduced before the game. A hush fell upon the 15,000 or so patrons, officials, and players in Maple Leaf Gardens.

Shore, normally a very confident and forceful man, seemed unsteady and uncertain as he tentatively stuck out his hand towards the bespectacled Bailey, who smiled broadly and firmly shook Shore's hand. Those in attendance cheered this shining display of sportsmanship.

The incidents that demonstrate Shore's toughness, his tenacity, and his ruthless demeanour are far more prevalent in the annals of hockey lore than those about his talents.

Although it took nearly a year after the Bailey incident to get back into his normal feisty fighting form, the next few years proved to be the most illustrious of Shore's career. He had been awarded the Hart Trophy as the NHL's most valuable player at the end of the 1932–1933 season, and was a first-team All-Star in 1931, 1932, and 1933.

After the Bailey hit, he still managed to be named a second-team All-Star in 1934. He won three more Hart Trophies (1935, 1936, and 1938), and was named to the first All-Star team in 1935, 1936, 1938, and 1939.

His swan song as a player came in the 1938–1939 campaign, when many observers — including his own manager, Art Ross — thought the 36 year old might be washed up. He may have slowed down a bit because of all the pounding his body took over the years, and he may have begun to lose more and more dust-ups to younger fighters looking to make a name for themselves, but after a couple of up-and-down seasons featuring some serious injuries, the wily old veteran played some of the best hockey of his career, particularly in the playoffs, where he set up key goals to eliminate the Rangers in the semi-finals. The Bruins then easily handled the Maple Leafs in the finals, prevailing in five games to win the Stanley Cup.

Shore and manager Art Ross had never really got along. Although acknowledging that he was a fine player, Ross didn't care much for Shore's independent nature. The defenceman was also old by hockey standards, and was becoming more inconsistent on the ice, notwithstanding his remarkable last couple of seasons.

Ross had been thinking about trading Shore for some time, hoping to get maximum value from the deal. Shore knew that his time in Boston was ending.

In the off-season, Shore announced that he had purchased the Springfield Indians of the then International American Hockey League (IAHL, later known simply as the AHL).

This move ticked off Ross, and made him even more

determined to trade his fading star. He felt that Shore would not be able to focus on the Bruins if he was trying to run the Indians. After four games in the 1939–1940 season, Shore was traded to the New York Americans for journeyman Ed Wiseman and $5,000 cash. He split his time between the Americans and the Indians.

The following season, he retired from the NHL to become the full-time playing coach for Springfield. It inaugurated the second half of the Shore legend — the quirky (some would say crazy) team owner who terrorized and underpaid hundreds of players for more than a quarter of a century.

Love him or hate him, Eddie Shore lived for hockey, and spent his entire lifetime in the sport. He was elected to the Hockey Hall of Fame in 1945.

Chapter 3
Ching Johnson: A Ranger Original

Hitting and grinning. Those are two of the things that Ching Johnson was best known for, and he was usually doing both at the same time. Johnson loved action, loved the physicality of the game, the one-on-one battles for supremacy that occurred dozens of times during a game.

One night in the early 1930s, the New York Rangers were playing the Montreal Maroons. Ching Johnson, defenceman for the Rangers, was in a particularly feisty mood. Hooley Smith was part of the top line for the Maroons during the late 1920s and early 1930s. A talented forward, he was a key cog on the team's famed Triple S Line, with Nels "Old Poison" Stewart and Babe Siebert. Smith also had a nasty temper.

On the Maroons' first rush up the ice, Smith was bearing

down on the Rangers' defence. He moved to Johnson's side. Johnson began to smile when he realized that Smith was looking down at the puck a little more than he should. An opportunity for mayhem — Johnson's adrenaline kicked up a notch.

Everyone in the league knew that Johnson loved body contact. Nothing gave him greater satisfaction on the ice than bashing into opponents and having them bash into him.

Smith should have known better, but he didn't. One of Johnson's teammates said the impact was so powerful that Smith's stick was knocked from his hands and flew almost as high as the arena lights. "[Smith] was lifted clean off the ice, and seemed to stay suspended five or six feet above the surface for seconds before finally crashing down on his back," said Johnson's teammate Frank Boucher.

Some perverse part of Smith's mind always had him rush at Johnson whenever he had the puck, refusing to believe that he could be on the losing end of every encounter with the tough defenceman. He was, and Johnson loved every minute of it.

Born Ivan Johnson in Winnipeg in 1898, Ching did not grow up playing hockey like most of his contemporaries. He loved many sports, but the passion for hockey blossomed only later in his childhood.

He played some hockey as a teenager, and returned to play his only season of junior hockey in Winnipeg after serving with the Canadian military during World War I. He then moved south to play semi-professional hockey, first in Eveleth, Minnesota, then in Minneapolis. Although Minneapolis is a major American city, it was still off the mainstream hockey map as far as most NHL teams were concerned.

In the mid-1920s, Johnson was "discovered" by the man contracted to bring a second big league hockey team to New York City — Conn Smythe.

In one of his earlier sojourns through the American Midwestern states, Smythe remembers a towering blueline duo playing for a semi-professional team in Minnesota.

Clarence "Taffy" Abel was 6'1" and 215 pounds; Johnson was shorter, but about the same weight, although he was far more densely packed. Abel was the better skater and passer, while Johnson could inflict some of the most powerful bodychecks Smythe had ever seen. Abel and Johnson would become the bedrock of the Rangers' defence.

Unfortunately for Smythe, he would never have the chance to coach Johnson. The Rangers soon fired him and replaced him with Lester Patrick.

An experienced player, coach, and manager, Patrick was eloquent in speech and patrician in manner. From the moment he held his first press conference in New York, Patrick became an instant celebrity — popular among the ink-stained wretches that made up the highly competitive New York print media.

It mattered not to Johnson who was running or coaching the team. He just wanted to play. Johnson made an immediate on-ice impact in the Rangers' first-ever NHL game, played on November 17, 1926. The Rangers, who counted only four players who had ever played big-league hockey, faced the powerhouse Montreal Maroons in Madison Square Garden.

Few gave the Rangers any chance. They were seen as being outclassed by the Maroons in both talent and toughness.

Nels Stewart, affectionately know as "Old Poison," was one of the toughest and most talented of the Montreal team. He decided he would dictate the tempo of the game from the get go and intimidate the blue-shirted upstarts.

Early in the game, the puck went behind the net of Rangers' goaltender, Lorne Chabot. Both Johnson and Stewart raced to get it. In the crash that ensued, Stewart got his stick up on Johnson, cutting him near the eye. Blood dripped onto the ice, and instead of writhing on the ice in pain, Johnson summarily knocked Stewart onto his backside. Johnson, while bloodied, was the only one standing.

Meanwhile Stewart's manoeuvre fired up both Johnson and the rest of the Rangers. "Ching was in his element, hoisting any Maroon body he could lay hip to, his face aglow in its grin, his bald head shining with sweat, and blood trickling from beneath the white [bandage] patch over his eye," said Boucher.

The Rangers won the game 1-0, and served notice on the entire league that they were a team to be reckoned with.

Johnson, Boucher, Chabot, and Bill and Bun Cook, along with the rest of the inaugural New York Rangers team, finished first in the newly formed American Division of the now 10-team NHL. Not only would the Rangers not be bullied, they were not prepared to be beaten either.

Ching Johnson began his second season in the NHL in fine fashion, scoring twice for the Rangers as they defeated the Toronto Maple Leafs 4-2 in Toronto. The Leafs were managed and coached by Conn Smythe — the man who was summarily spurned by the Rangers organization.

Johnson no doubt delighted in tweaking the nose of his former boss, as he helped the Rangers to the second-best record in the five-team American Division; the Rangers' record was 10-8-5 for 25 points, just one back of the Boston Bruins. By the end of the season, the Rangers were still in second spot behind Boston, but only one point up on the Pittsburgh Pirates, and three ahead of the Detroit Red Wings.

Johnson was tied for 16th place in league scoring, with 10 goals and 6 assists over a 42-game schedule. That's a significant point tally, considering the overall points leader in the entire NHL, Howie Morenz of the Canadiens, had 51, and his linemate, Aurel Joliat, was second with 39. In fact, Johnson was the fourth-highest point producer on the Rangers that season, while accumulating 146 penalty minutes.

The playoffs opened with the Rangers hosting Pittsburgh. The series would feature a goaltending duel between Lorne Chabot of New York and Roy Worters of the Pirates.

With Johnson, Abel, and their blueline backups, the Rangers boasted the largest defence corps in the league, averaging 225 pounds. Johnson was its leader, both for his enthusiasm on the ice and his take-charge, rah-rah manner in the dressing room.

Pittsburgh also boasted a tough team, with defencemen such as Herb Drury and Harold "Baldy" Cotton, as well as the talented Hib Milks and Harold Darragh up front. However, the Pirates came out flat and the Rangers toyed with them. Although Johnson was considered a mediocre skater, he registered a few dangerous rushes into enemy territory and scored in the second period of the game. The game ended 4-0.

The Pirates decided to get rough in the second game. Before it ended, both Abel (clipped with a high stick) and Frank Boucher were knocked out of the match. Without Boucher's effective forechecking, and without Abel complementing Johnson, the Pirates pillaged the Rangers to the tune of 4-2. Since this was a two-game, total-goals series, New York advanced to the next round on a 6-4 aggregate.

In the semi-finals, it was a match-up that hockey fans had been anticipating — the New York Rangers against the first-place Bruins. But more importantly, fans had a chance to see Ching Johnson go *mano a mano* with Boston's tough and talented defender Eddie Shore.

Even though they were both blueliners, Shore was known for his willingness to grab the puck and run with it. Johnson, as he had proved in the series against Pittsburgh, was no slouch in the rushing department either. This meant there were many opportunities for the two roughnecks to rumble.

This, also, was a two-game, total-goals series. In the first game, Shore and Johnson each received four minor penalties for infractions committed against the other. The game ended in a 1-1 draw, with Shore and Johnson glaring at one another as each skated off the ice. In the second game, a number of key Bruins were either out with injuries, or playing hurt, and the Rangers stormed through a weakened Bruins defence. Shore was busy chasing around Boucher and the Cook brothers, while Johnson was content to play his usual robust defensive style. New York won the second game 4-1, and the total goals series 5-2.

The finals would be between the Rangers and the Montreal Maroons. The Rangers carried much of the play, but lost the series opener 2-0. In the second game, with the teams tied at 0-0, Rangers' goalie, Lorne Chabot, took a puck to the face and was finished for the game. Montreal would not allow the Rangers to use one of the available netminders who happened to be on hand, so manager Lester Patrick donned the pads himself and played goal for the rest of the game.

Bill Cook scored in the third period to make it 1-0 Rangers, while Johnson and the rest of the team literally threw themselves at the Maroons, gobbling up their scoring rushes, and preventing as many shots as possible from getting in on the man who signed their paycheques.

Nels Stewart, one of the most dangerous goal scorers in league history, did manage to beat Patrick, sending the game into overtime. Then, at the 7:50 mark, Boucher beat the Maroons' outstanding netminder, Clint Benedict, with a hard shot that came after Johnson managed to keep the puck in the offensive zone after some scrambly play. Boucher was the hero of the game, but many gave credit to Johnson for getting the puck to Boucher through traffic.

In the third game, backup netminder Joe Miller was no match for the Maroons, who took a 2-1 series lead on Benedict's second shutout.

In the next game, Johnson and Abel were back to their stifling, stiff-arming best, preventing little in the way of a co-ordinated Maroons' attack to get in on Miller. Because Miller was not a front-line NHL goalie like Lorne Chabot, Patrick determined the way to win was to do everything to protect Miller and to capitalize on any breaks they got offensively. A power-play tally by Boucher, who tapped in an unusually juicy rebound off Benedict's pads, was all the Rangers needed to tie the series.

Frank Boucher was the star of the series on offence for the Rangers, scoring both goals in a 2-1 Stanley Cup-clinching win. Johnson, playing with an incredible amount of intensity and belligerence, had two points in the nine playoff games, as well as 46 penalty minutes to lead all players in the post season.

Johnson and the Rangers remained at or near the top of

the league for much of the early 1930s. The core of Johnson, Boucher, the Cook brothers, plus Cecil Dillon and goalie John Ross Roach remained intact under the tutelage of the Silver Fox, Lester Patrick.

Although it took a few years, Conn Smythe had his revenge on the organization that unceremoniously turfed him. In the 1932 Stanley Cup finals — the first one to be played in the new Maple Leaf Gardens — Smythe's Maple Leafs, with former Ranger Lorne Chabot in goal; King Clancy and Hap Day on defence; and the Kid Line of Busher Jackson, Joe Primeau, and Charlie Conacher up front — outworked, outfought, and outscored the Rangers to win the Cup.

But the Rangers were simply too good a team, with too many weapons, to not rebound. Heading into the 1932–1933 season, Johnson and Abel still anchored the defence in front of new goalie, Andy Aitkenhead, who had replaced John Ross Roach. The Cooks and Boucher still paced the New York attack.

The Rangers made the playoffs and faced the Canadiens in the opening round. Johnson and new partner Earl Seibert kept the powerful Montreal offence, and particularly superstar centre Howie Morenz, at bay, limiting the number of scoring chances goaltender Aitkenhead would have to face. The Rangers' top line of the Cooks and Boucher was much better than the Morenz, Aurel Joliat, Johnny Gagnon combo, helping New York to a 5-2 win in the series opener.

In the second game of this two-game, total-goals

encounter, back in Montreal, the tables were turned, as Montreal stormed the New Yorkers, for a 3-0 lead. But Johnson and the rest of the Rangers stepped up their defensive play, while Cecil Dillon scored twice in the last two minutes of the game to give the Rangers the round 8-5.

The next series, against Detroit, saw Ching Johnson at his bashing best. The Detroit defence was so porous that Johnson rushed in from centre ice for the first goal of the game. The Rangers won that contest 2-0, and Johnson's overall play generated great press in New York newspapers.

Detroit clamped down on defence, and ramped up the rough play in the second game of the series. Johnson was keeping the Falcons at bay, until Ebbie Goodfellow, whose name belied his violent actions that night, chopped him in the head. While Johnson was in getting repairs, Detroit began to light up the goal lamp. Ultimately, Johnson's return and Dillon's great offensive play carried the game and the series for New York.

For the second time in two years, Conn Smythe would have a chance to show the owners of the Rangers that they had made a grave error in letting him slip away. The year before, his Maple Leafs had swept aside the Rangers in three straight games, and a confident Smythe expected to repeat the performance.

The tired Maple Leafs (they had eliminated the Bruins less than 12 hours earlier in one of the longest games in NHL history) fell 5-1 in the opening game of this best-of-five tilt. Johnson played well, but was overshadowed by his partner, Seibert, who stole a page from his mentor's book by rushing through the entire Toronto team to score a goal in the second game of the series, garnering the Rangers a 3-1 victory.

The Leafs salvaged some pride by winning the next game 3-2, but ultimately couldn't hold back Dillon and the rest of the Ranger forwards. Veteran Bill Cook scored the Cup-winning goal in a 1-0 game four win for New York.

The New York Rangers had won their second Stanley Cup in only their seventh year of existence.

Not only had they won, but they had done it with a combination of the old guard and younger players. Seibert had begun to supplant Johnson, while Dillon had taken over from the Cooks and Boucher as the top offensive threat on the Rangers. They could all see the writing on the wall, but were happy to be part of this transition, which would hopefully see the Rangers — the team they helped birth — stay at the top for many years to come.

By the end of the 1936–1937 season, the Rangers thanked Johnson for his efforts with the club, but said his services were no longer needed. A youth movement was now in full swing. Clint Smith, Bryan Hextall, and Alex Shibicky were just three of the younger players brought in to play alongside the few remaining veterans.

Johnson figured he still had a few more crunching bodychecks in him, so he decided to try his luck with another

NHL team. He simply walked down the hall to the dressing room and offices of the rival New York Americans, and asked their manager, Red Dutton, for a job.

Earlier on, Dutton had decided that the best course of action for the Americans was to squeeze every last drop of talent, energy, and experience out of a handful of veterans who nobody else wanted, and mix in a dose of young blood. Johnson joined a team that already included the likes of Hooley Smith, Nels "Old Poison" Stewart, and Hap Day.

Both New York teams played well that 1937–1938 season, exceeding expectations. The Americans finished second in the Canadian Division, while the Rangers were second in the American Division, so for the first time in their combined histories, the two New York teams would square off in a playoff series.

The teams split the first two hard-fought games, and had the same number of goals. The series would be decided by a sudden-death third game. In one of the longest games in league history, Americans utility forward Art Jerwa beat the Rangers' goaltender, Davey Kerr, to win the series.

Throughout the series, Johnson's solid play belied his advancing years, a fact not lost on Lester Patrick, the man who cut him loose. At the end of the game, Patrick hopped onto the ice and hollered for his former defenceman to come over. Patrick shook his hand and complimented Johnson on a great series, wishing him luck against Chicago in the next round.

Johnson retired from the NHL after his one, injury-plagued season with the Americans. He returned to Minnesota, and suited up for his former team in Minneapolis for two seasons before moving into the coaching ranks. He was inducted into the Hockey Hall of Fame in 1958.

Chapter 4
Dit Clapper:
Class and Longevity

t was only when Dit Clapper decided to hang up his blades for good that he realized just how well respected he was by his teammates and peers, and how much of an impact he had had on the NHL.

Clapper decided that two consecutive decades of punishing hits, sticks to the face, gruelling practices, and endless miles of skating were enough. All 20 years of his remarkable career had been played in Boston with the Bruins, which at the time was the longest tenure of any player on one team in the history of the sport. It was also the longest consecutive tenure of any player in the NHL itself: two seasons longer than the previous mark of 18 seasons, held by Hooley Smith.

Clapper was a tenacious checker who gave everything

he had on the ice, but also left it there. Whatever problems he had with officials or opponents were forgotten when the game was over. He was not a bombastic showman like his mercurial teammate, Eddie Shore. He didn't score flashy goals like his contemporary, King Clancy. He excelled at the overall game of hockey. He did everything very, very well. There were few holes in his game, and his versatility, talent, passion, longevity, and class made him one of the most popular players of his day — a popularity that lasted well into his retirement.

Aubrey Victor Clapper, born in the southern Ontario town of Newmarket in 1907, was raised in several Ontario towns. Like most kids growing up in Canada at that time, sports were a key part of Clapper's life.

His father, William Clapper, had grown up near Peterborough in the small village of Hastings, and was one of the region's best lacrosse players. Son Aubrey inherited his dad's athleticism and physical endurance. He followed in his footsteps, and at one point, father and teenaged son played together on a provincial championship team.

One particular incident shows how the seemingly mutually exclusive traits of toughness and classiness were passed from father to son. The Clappers were in a heated lacrosse match that featured a great deal of rough play. At one point, the younger Clapper took a hard shot to the head from an opponent's stick and was knocked out. Bill Clapper proceeded to mete out a little bit of fatherly justice by knocking out his offender with a shot to his noggin.

To the delight of the crowd, the elder Clapper first revived his son and teammate, and then went over to revive the opponent, making sure he was all right.

As good a lacrosse player as he was — and by all accounts he was as talented as his old man — it was as a hockey player that Dit Clapper would find his true calling.

He learned to skate on frozen ponds and rivers in and around Hastings, and played pick-up games on outdoor rinks. After moving to Aurora, he played in both the school league and local church leagues as a 12 and 13 year old. He generated enough acclaim on the ice to be invited at the remarkably youthful age of 14 to join a junior team in Oshawa.

Clapper was growing into a strapping young lad 6'2" and closing in on 200 pounds. While that's about the size of an average NHL player today, back in the 1920s he was considered to be a mountain of a man and was put on defence.

By the time he moved up to the Toronto Parkdale junior team in 1925, he was known as a tough but clean body-checker who effectively neutralized the opposing team's best forwards. But he also displayed superior skating ability and a talent for handling and shooting the puck. Scouts with the Boston Bruins' organization took note of his playmaking abilities, as well as his size, strength, and work ethic.

Former NHL coach Eddie Powers was coaching the Boston Tigers, the main minor league affiliate of the Bruins, when he came to Toronto to scout Clapper. He was so impressed, he signed the 18 year old to a contract.

In one season with the Tigers, Clapper showed that he was a tough player who didn't instigate fights, but could defend himself if provoked. He racked up 57 penalty minutes in 29 games, and also added six goals, a respectable tally in an age when defencemen rarely made offensive forays. He was tagged to play with the big club the following year.

It didn't take legendary Bruins manager/coach Art Ross long to see the benefits of moving Clapper up to the forward line. He was already well stocked with talented, tough-minded defencemen, such as Eddie Shore and Lionel Hitchman. He felt Clapper's skating ability, shooting and passing skills, as well as his size and strength, would be an asset to the team's offence. So Clapper became a forward.

He scored only four goals in his rookie NHL season, seeing spot duty as a 19 year old. He bumped his total up to nine goals for the 1928–1929 season. That year, the Bruins were the dominant team in the NHL, winning the Stanley Cup for the first time in team history.

Then Ross decided that Clapper would be a nice fit as the right winger on a line with centre Norm "Dutch" Gainor, and sophomore scoring ace Cooney Weiland. That season, the three of them exploded onto the score sheets of the NHL, supplying 102 of the team's 179 goals. With the newly minted Dynamite Line up front, the defensive corps led by the bruising tandem of Shore and Hitchman, and the brilliant netminding of Cecil "Tiny" Thompson, Boston compiled the best winning percentage in the history of the NHL. The team won 38 games, lost only 5, and tied 1.

Unfortunately, the Montreal Canadiens, though aging, still had Howie Morenz and Aurel Joliat up front, with George Hainsworth between the pipes. They upended the Bruins in the playoffs, en route to the Stanley Cup.

Throughout the 1930s, the Bruins were always in the thick of things in the playoffs but couldn't seem to put the magic formula together. Ross brought in younger players, keeping a nucleus that was centred around Eddie Shore, and even more, the classy Clapper. Shore was a great player, but he was individualistic, stand-offish, and prone to fits of mayhem. Clapper was steady and elegant. He had enough toughness and talent to earn respect, without invoking fear and hatred.

Clapper was not only a hero in the hockey arena, but in real life as well. Every fall, just before hockey season, Clapper liked to get in a little duck hunting. An avid sportsman, Clapper's aim was as good with a rifle or shotgun as it was with a hockey stick. One October in the mid-1930s, he and three pals were out on the Trent River near Peterborough, Ontario, looking for supper on the wing. The river began to get rough as a wind kicked up, and the canoe with the four men was swamped, throwing all of them into the frigid water.

Soaked to the bone and clinging to the canoe, the four men shivered and grew weaker by the minute. Clapper realized something had to be done. He managed to remove his heavy jackets and sweaters, his hip waders and pants, and

Dit Clapper

then, after exhorting his companions to hold on to the canoe and not give up, he swam half a mile to shore. He found a small rowboat, untied it from its moorings, and quickly rowed it back to the capsized canoe. He dragged his three shivering friends into the rowboat and returned them to shore, safe and sound.

Throughout his career, Clapper was known as an honest, classy player who rarely lost his temper or deliberately tried to injure an opponent. This reputation worked in his favour in the aftermath of a disturbing incident in his otherwise glorious career.

Dave Trottier was a left winger with the Montreal Maroons, who had impressive offensive numbers to go along with a fair number of minutes racked up in the penalty box. By the time the 1937 playoffs rolled around, he was nearing the end of his career, and the Maroons were only a year away from dropping out of the NHL.

The Maroons, from the time they entered the league, were a tough team known for occasionally using nasty tactics to achieve their victories. Early in the series between the Maroons and Bruins, Trottier tangled with a young Boston player, and decided to disentangle himself from the rookie by slamming him in the face with the butt end of his stick. The Boston player went down in a crumpled heap. Showing a side of his character that rarely surfaced, Clapper raced over to Trottier, and pummeled him with fists, knocking him out. But Clapper didn't stop there; he jumped on the Maroon player's prone, bloodied body and kept pounding.

The players from both teams must have been stunned to see the normally gentlemanly Clapper reduced to such barbarism, because no player from either team stepped in to stem the assault. It fell upon the referee to intervene. As he attempted to wrestle Clapper off Trottier, the ref uttered a few uncomplimentary epithets at the veteran Bruin. He finally resorted to grabbing him by the hair and dragging him off.

Clapper, still incensed beyond reason, punched the referee in the face, knocking the official onto his backside. The official's name was Clarence Campbell, a man who would go on to be part of the prosecution team behind the Nuremburg war crimes trials and a future president of the NHL.

Everyone in the league, especially officials with the Maroons, called for a heavy penalty, such as expulsion for the rest of the season. But Campbell went to bat for Clapper in his hearing with NHL president Frank Calder. "I called Clapper a name that angered him. I was wrong to do so," he told Calder, asking for leniency for Clapper. The Boston star, to the chagrin of the Maroons, received only a one-game suspension and a $100 fine.

Later that fall, with the emergence of energetic, talented young forwards Bobby Bauer, Woody Dumart, and Milt Schmidt, Clapper was asked to move back to defence, where he remained for the rest of his stellar career. He was initially paired with the bombastic, but incredibly effective Eddie Shore, making one of the most potent and feared defensive duos in the history of the league.

The Bruins fell to second in the American Division at the end of the 1936–1937 season, but were back on top the following year — Clapper's first on the blueline. However, the underdog Chicago Blackhawks, who finished 30 points behind the Bruins in the standings, won the Stanley Cup that year.

With Clapper and Shore leading the way from the blueline and new scoring star Bill Cowley leading the offensive charge, Boston topped the league in 1938–1939 by 16 points over the second-place New York Rangers. Clapper had come into his own as a blueliner and helped give the Bruins the stingiest defence in the entire league.

Boston allowed a paltry 76 goals that season. The Rangers were next best in that department, surrendering 105 tallies. Clapper's performance was so brilliant that for the first time, he was named to the NHL First All-Star Team — as a defenceman. He had been a Second Team All-Star twice before as a forward. It would mark the first of his three consecutive nominations to the First Team.

Clapper almost ended his career in November of that year. His pal and roommate, the great goaltender Cecil "Tiny" Thompson, had been sold to Detroit and replaced by the up-and-coming youngster Frank Brimsek. Clapper, in a rare fit of pique, told Bruins' management of his displeasure, arguing that if Tiny was no longer good enough to be a Bruin, then maybe he wasn't either.

Cooler heads prevailed, and Clapper eventually conceded that Ross had actually made a very shrewd move. Brimsek turned out to be every bit as good as his predecessor, earning the nickname Mr. Zero for registering 231 minutes and 54 seconds of shutout goaltending. He also earned the Calder Trophy as the league's top rookie and the Vezina Trophy as the top netminder.

That season, the Rangers would be Boston's first round

opponent and would fall under the spell of "Sudden Death" Mel Hill. While Shore and Clapper held up their end of the ice, keeping Rangers' shooters at bay in front of Brimsek, the Boston offence was somewhat stifled. The Rangers blanketed Cowley and Roy Conacher, but their checking linemate, Mel Hill, was unmarked. Ross told the two offensive dynamos to look for Hill in the open. It worked. Hill scored three sudden death overtime goals to propel the Bruins to the finals. But not before Clapper's cool head came to the fore.

In the fourth game of this highly combative series, Lynn Patrick clubbed Eddie Shore over the head with his stick, knocking the veteran out of the game. A brawl ensued, and the fiery rookie goalie Brimsek raced toward Patrick, looking to wreak a little revenge. Fortunately for Brimsek and the Bruins, Clapper saw him coming, and grabbed Frankie before he got himself hurt, penalized, or both.

The series stretched to a wearying seven games, with Mel Hill the eventual hero. After this war, the finals against the Maple Leafs were a dawdle, as Boston waltzed to their second Stanley Cup. It was also Clapper's second.

The Bruins finished first overall again the next season, even without Eddie Shore, who had moved on to the New York Americans. The Bruins held the first four positions in the overall scoring race, while Clapper picked up his second nod to the First All-Star Team. But the Rangers were also an improved team. This would be their year, as they won their third Cup in less than a decade. It was the last time the

Rangers won Lord Stanley's mug, until captain Mark Messier would hoist it 54 years later.

The following season, the Bruins rebounded to again win the league title, and then move, with frightening efficiency, through the playoffs to the finals, where they captured the team's second Stanley Cup in three seasons, and third in 10 years.

Dit Clapper was on top of the world. He was now a three-time Stanley Cup champion, and the first (and still only) player in NHL history to be named a First Team All-Star as a forward and a defenceman. That would be a great career for many players if it ended right there, and it almost did for Clapper.

In a game against the Toronto Maple Leafs, late in the 1941–1942 season, Clapper had his Achilles tendon cut by an errant skate blade of the Leafs' Bingo Kampman during a wild scramble. For any athlete, this is a devastating injury.

Usually, when athletes tear or sever this critical tendon, like Achilles of Greek mythology, their days of being a hero are over. It seemed this would be the case for Dit Clapper.

"It required 100 stitches inside and another 100 stitches outside the wound," said son Don. "The doctors said he might never skate again, that he'd be lucky to be able to walk. Well, he was back on skates the following year."

While some press reports claim he was never the same player he was before the injury, he was still a key offensive and defensive contributor, and made the NHL Second All-

Star Team after the 1943–1944 season.

Before the start of the next season, he was named head coach of the Bruins, added to his duties as the team's longtime captain.

Even Clapper realized that the sands of time were running out on his career. He played 30 games that season, and then only six at the start of the 1946–1947 season. He didn't officially announce his retirement as a player for a few months. Shortly after the announcement, it was decided that he would be the centre of attention at a special pre-game ceremony at the Boston Garden on February 12, 1947.

Even Wayne Gretzky was not feted the way Clapper was that emotional night at the Garden. Besides receiving thousands of dollars' worth of gifts from representatives of all six NHL teams, the league itself, and from representatives of the Bruins' fans, he also received a plaque signifying his immediate induction into the Hockey Hall of Fame.

To this day, he is the only active player to receive such an honour. He was still technically registered as a player until the end of the season. When the ceremonies began, Clapper had suited up in his uniform with the familiar Number 5 and skated out with the rest of his teammates.

After the heart-warming festivities and with nary a dry eye in the building, Clapper saluted the crowd and went back to the Bruins dressing room to change into his street clothes. Then he took his place behind the bench.

Tributes to Clapper came from far and wide.

"He played hard always. But once [the game] was over, he held no enmity. That's what made him great too, made him popular with other players, with other fans in other cities," wrote Bobby Hewitson, a sports columnist and former NHL referee.

"He had been a fine hockey player, a fine model for young hockeyists breaking in and he has become a good coach ...," penned a scribe in the *Montreal Star*.

"We salute you as one of the most courageous, gifted, and sportsmanlike rivals we have ever met," were comments coming from Chicago Blackhawks' management.

Leave it to the inimitable Conn Smythe to offer up the wisest of cracks and take a swipe at the man he disliked most in hockey. "Anybody who works 20 years for Art Ross definitely belongs in the Hall of Fame," he said.

The esteem to which Clapper was held in Boston was no more evident than during the fall of 1983. Bruins' manager Harry Sinden had signed free agent defenceman Guy Lapointe, a multi-time All-Star and Stanley Cup winner with Montreal. Lapointe had always worn Number 5 on his jersey, even after he left Montreal for a two-year stint in St. Louis. He wanted to wear his familiar number with the Bruins. But Number 5 was Dit Clapper's number, and the team had retired it in 1947.

Sinden was desperate to improve his floundering team, and was going to acquiesce to Lapointe's demand, for fear of offending the player he had just signed. There was universal outrage in the media, inside and outside of Boston. How could Sinden so shamelessly throw aside a large part of the early history of the franchise to placate a former rival?

"Listen Harry: Dit Clapper richly deserved his hockey immortality. Let him rest in peace. And let his No. 5 hang forever from the steel beams of Boston Garden ...," wrote veteran sportswriter Jim Coleman, a sentiment echoed by the acerbic Boston writer Leo Monahan.

"It's ghoulish what Sinden's done to Clapper," Monahan told Toronto sportswriter Dick Beddoes. "It's robbing the grave. It's defiling a decent man who entered the Hall of Fame through the front door ...."

Harold Ballard, the cranky, publicity-seeking owner of the Maple Leafs got in on the act, too. "They make enough fuss when they retire one. Are they telling us that retiring Clapper's number didn't mean anything?"

But the straw that broke Sinden's back was comments by another player who had his number retired by the Bruins, not long after Clapper died. "If they're going to unretire Number 5, which honours a Bruin who gave so much to the game, they might as well unretire Number 4," said Bobby Orr.

Lapointe soon found himself wearing Number 27, and Sinden realized that, for a player who exhibited such class, leadership and loyalty to an organization, there will always be people making sure the fine, gentlemanly legacy of Dit Clapper is preserved for all time.

That legacy goes beyond the numbers. Yes, he scored

Dit Clapper: Class and Longevity

228 goals and totalled 246 points, while spending more than half his career as a defenceman, but it is the class and dignity with which he carried himself, the way he never carried a grudge beyond the final whistle, and his work ethic, talent, grace, and skill for which he will be best remembered.

Chapter 5
Doug Harvey: Montreal's Rock of Gibraltar

From the moment Doug Harvey pulled on the red, white, and blue uniform of the Montreal Canadiens as a raw rookie in the 1947–1948 season, the emotions of fans, coaches, and media alike vacillated between jaw-dropping awe and blind fury, exultation and utter frustration.

For the first few years, most people didn't know what to make of him. He seemed lazy. There was no urgency in many of his breakout plays; he made dangerously long, last-minute passes; and he lingered too long with the puck in front of his own net.

It was enough to make coach Dick Irvin Sr. want to pull his hair out — until he realized the plays were part of Harvey's genius.

Doug Harvey: Montreal's Rock of Gibraltar

Never had a player been able to dominate the tone and tempo of a game from the blueline before. Never had a player possessed such a potent combination of skills: incredible natural athletic ability, great vision for the game, an unmatched instinct for how a play would develop, strength, skating ability, frighteningly accurate passing, quiet leadership, and humility. Doug Harvey was the complete package.

In the last game of his rookie season in the 1947–1948 campaign, fans, teammates, and Irvin were treated to a glimpse of Harvey's team-first mentality in a game where the only thing on the line was a scoring title for popular forward Elmer Lach.

The Canadiens had already conceded the fourth and final playoff spot to the New York Rangers, so the scoring title was the only thing of significance to attain.

Lach was tied with Rangers' Buddy O'Connor at 60 points. The Rangers had completed their schedule, so there was no way for O'Connor to break the tie.

Late in the game, with Montreal already assured a victory, Harvey grabbed the puck deep in his own zone. Instead of the seemingly sluggish way he had been playing for much of the year, and for which he endured great criticism, Harvey burst through his zone, past the blueline — a red, white, and blue blur as he passed opponents and teammates alike.

Lach was up ahead and saw his young teammate streaking up the ice, hell bent for the other team's goal. Everyone in the building thought he would shoot the puck, knowing that he had a hard and accurate shot.

Instead, he made a move to deke the goaltender way out of his crease, leaving a huge hole to put the puck in.

Without uttering a word, he simply slid the puck to the place where he instinctively knew Lach was going to be. Lach tapped the puck in the near-empty cage for his 61st point of the season, and his second and last scoring championship. While it was his second title, Harvey and the rest of his team-mates knew that the winner of the scoring title would be the first NHL player to receive the new Art Ross Trophy as the league's top point producer.

Harvey used his brilliance and his talent not to forward his own ambitions or get his name in the headlines that night. He wanted his teammate to succeed and the rest of the boys in the dressing room to feel good about what was otherwise a lost season. With that attitude in place, Harvey became a key part of a Canadiens' rebuilding movement.

Harvey grew up in a hard-working, hard-drinking part of Montreal. A natural athlete from the time he could walk, he starred in baseball, football, and boxing.

He played all manner of sports until he joined the Navy. While playing for the Navy hockey team during World War II, he did double duty with the Montreal Junior Royals — part of the Montreal Canadiens' expansive farm system. He impressed coaches so much that he was called up for a game with the Senior Royals.

Canadiens' officials heard reports of the way he could pass, shoot, and skate, befuddling veteran Senior League players and goaltenders. He became known for playing seemingly limitless amounts of time, while often controlling the game.

But Harvey was also seen as a bit unorthodox. He hesitated a lot before making an outlet pass and would often carry the puck out of the corner in front of his own net. He sometimes seemed disinterested and too relaxed.

He was also tough. Although generally even-tempered at this early part of his hockey career, Harvey displayed flashes of aggression. In his final year of senior hockey, he accumulated a league record of 171 penalty minutes.

In that 1947–1948 season, Harvey played 24 games with Buffalo of the AHL before coming up to the Habs, where he notched eight goals and eight assists in 35 games — heady numbers at the time for a rookie defenceman in the NHL.

Harvey wasn't a star right out of the chute. He was growing into his role as a solid NHL contributor, but the quirks of his game were still unpolished, and he still caused grief for coach Dick Irvin because of his unique style and relaxed demeanour.

In Harvey's second season, Irvin criticized him for carrying the puck too much and for too long, especially late in the game. But Harvey's notion was that it was silly to just give the puck away for little gain, instead of looking and waiting for the best possible pass out of the zone.

Irvin became so concerned over Harvey's tendency to

skate with the puck in front of his own net that he threatened to fine him $100 (at the time Harvey was only making around $6,000 per season.) if the opposing team checked the puck off him and scored. Irvin never had to pay up, but for a few years, teammates would refer to the area around the Montreal goal crease as "Doug's $100 Zone."

Harvey was part of a cast of characters that was coalescing around superstar Maurice Richard in the early 1950s. Boom Boom Geoffrion, goalie Jacques Plante, and others had come on board, and by the 1952–1953 season, Montreal was back as a Stanley Cup contender.

It's easy to be a hero when everything is going well, but the measure of a man is how he reacts to adversity. That season, the Canadiens were mired in a slump. It was February, and games were starting to become more and more important. One night, when a two-goal lead disappeared and the team lost, manager Frank Selke and coach Irvin both thought Harvey was the main reason for the poor performance. So in the next game, against Toronto, Irvin benched him — the one and only time it ever happened in his career. Even at the end of the game, when the score was 1-0 for Montreal and fans were calling out Harvey's name, Irvin kept him planted at the end of the Habs' bench.

Harvey took his punishment silently, without protest. The next night against Detroit, he took his regular shift, as he did for the rest of the season. He was voted to the NHL First All-Star Team, and was a key player in the Canadiens' Stanley

Cup win later that spring — the first of six he would win wearing a Habs uniform.

The following year, a man of lesser character and confidence would have been shattered by what had happened in the most pivotal moment of the Stanley Cup campaign. The Canadiens were locked in a life and death struggle with the powerhouse Detroit Red Wings in the finals. The Red Wings had finished atop the NHL standings and boasted one of the most potent offences in the league, led by Gordie Howe, Ted Lindsay up front, and Harvey's main rival for top league blueliner honours, Leonard "Red" Kelly.

The game was tied 1-1 at the end of regulation time in the seventh game. Whoever scored in overtime would win the Stanley Cup.

Harvey was on the ice, as he had been for more than half the game, in front of goaltender Gerry McNeil. The Wings were in the middle of a line change when Tony Leswick got the puck after a Harvey clearing attempt.

Leswick carried the puck just inside the Montreal blueline, and when Rocket Richard charged towards him, he fired a wrist shot in the general direction of McNeil.

Leswick had a fairly weak shot, and Harvey planned to "palm" the puck, drop it to his stick, and get rid of it. Instead, the puck deflected off Harvey's glove and evaded a flummoxed McNeil.

Harvey obviously felt bad but didn't fall to pieces. He simply rededicated himself to playing the best hockey he possibly could. The following season, Harvey won the first of his seven Norris Trophies as the NHL's top defenceman. From 1955–1956 on, he was an integral part of the most powerful hockey machine to grace an NHL arena, as the mighty Montreal Canadiens won five consecutive Stanley Cups. Harvey won his first Norris Trophy in 1955.

While he rarely scored more than six goals in a season, Harvey routinely was one of the league's leading defencemen in assists and points. His vision on the ice allowed him to make incredibly accurate passes, most of the time when the intended target was in full flight. And Harvey made it seem so easy, as though he were doing it for the pure enjoyment of the play.

Doug Harvey was known as being light-hearted — a jokester — the one who would keep everyone loose in the dressing room. He never seemed to take a defeat too hard or celebrate too much when he won. But there was still the heart of a true competitor, and a temper under that smiling, "aw shucks" demeanour.

Scrappy New York Ranger centre Red Sullivan found that out the hard way in a game played against the Canadiens in Madison Square Garden. Sullivan had gained a reputation for kicking skates. He would move toward an opposing player, and then when the moment was right, he would literally kick the opposing player's feet out from under him. Many injuries occurred because of this move.

At the Forum in the first of a home-and-home series with the Rangers, Sullivan used the move on Harvey. When

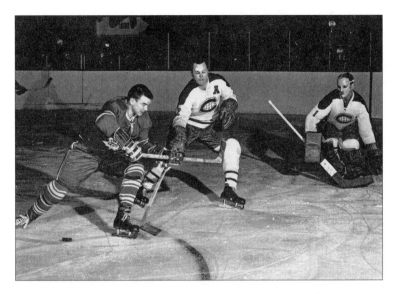

Doug Harvey (centre) poke checks the puck as
Jacques Plante gets prepared to make a save.

the defenceman rose to his feet, he skated near Sullivan and
gave him a not-so-subtle warning. Most players took a warning from Doug Harvey seriously, since he was not known for
making idle threats.

Harvey was also upset because Sullivan kept running
into Montreal netminder Jacques Plante whenever the tender
wandered from his crease.

Incredibly, Sullivan again kicked out Harvey's skates
near the end of the game. Harvey did not retaliate in the
game on home ice. Instead, he decided to wait for the return
match in New York, the following night.

When Sullivan pulled the move on Harvey in Madison Square Garden, the burly blueliner got up quickly, found the target of his rage, and speared Sullivan in the gut with a hard jab. Sullivan yelped, fell to the ice, and rolled around in obvious agony. No one knew how serious the injury was until he was wheeled off the ice and taken to a nearby hospital. His spleen had been ruptured, and there was serious concern for the life of Red Sullivan. Harvey was unrepentant and didn't complain when the league punished him.

In his autobiography, teammate and friend Boom Boom Geoffrion described the importance of Harvey to the Canadiens' dynasty of the late 1950s. "Doug was in his prime and there wasn't a better defenceman anywhere. He controlled the game like an orchestra conductor. When he wanted to speed up the tempo, he'd dash from his end to the other one and set up a play. Likewise, he could slow down the pace just as easily by taking the puck and lazily moving it around until the speed was to his liking."

The Canadiens won the Cup for the second straight time in 1957, and made it a three-peat in 1958. Harvey had one of the finest post-seasons ever by a defenceman. In game six of the finals that year, the Canadiens were up three games to Boston's two. It was 4-1 in the third period, until the plucky Boston team rallied to score twice, making it 4-3.

Then Bruins' coach Milt Schmidt pulled goaltender Don Simmons for an extra attacker. The action was fast and furious in the Montreal end. Harvey had been on the ice for practically the entire third period, but seemed as fresh as at the start of the game.

Unruffled by the intense action and extreme emotion of the situation, he intercepted a pass and headed deliberately up the ice with the puck. Boston player Larry Regan was playing "goal" in place of Simmons, who was sitting on the bench. Harvey shot the puck from a fair distance out, and Regan made the save, but Harvey kept skating and blasted the rebound in for a 5-3 final, putting an exclamation mark on the game and the series.

Harvey was fearless on the ice, which is why he could confidently skate up the ice and leave his defensive position at such a critical juncture in the game. Harvey's fearlessness also led him to come to the defence of a referee late in his tenure with the Canadiens.

It was the sixth game of the 1959 Stanley Cup semifinals between the Habs and the Blackhawks. With less than five minutes remaining in the third period, the game was tied 4-4, and referee Red Storey had nailed Chicago defender Al Arbour with a two-minute penalty. This angered the home crowd, but the emotion abated when Chicago managed to kill off the infraction. Seconds after Arbour returned to the ice, a Montreal defenceman nailed Bobby Hull with a hip check that fans thought should have been deemed a trip.

Figuring that Storey owed them one for Arbour's penalty, they became unhinged when Storey didn't call the perceived infraction. The place bordered on bedlam when Claude Provost scored to make it 5-4 for Montreal.

Garbage of all types began flying through the air in the direction of Storey. Mob mentality kicked in, and trash littered the ice.

Wisely, Storey moved to centre ice.

"So I'm at centre ice and all of a sudden somebody yells at me to look out. I turn around and this guy had come off the Chicago bench, a fan. He threw one of those plastic cups of beer right in my puss. I grabbed him. I was so teed off, I was really going to clean his clock," Storey told sportswriter Red Fisher.

Harvey was the one who yelled the warning. He too grabbed the fan, and for a moment it looked as though Storey and Harvey were going to turn the fan into a human wishbone. But Harvey, seeing that Storey was about to smack the offending fan, yelled at him not to do it. When Storey didn't let go, Harvey told him again that it would be career suicide for an official to hit a fan.

The moment Storey released the fan, Harvey hit the offender with a solid shot to the mouth. After a second punch, the fan staggered off the ice. Immediately, another fan charged at Storey and Harvey told Storey to duck.

"Here's this guy in mid-air about to jump on my back, so the ol' redhead dipped a little. The guy is off his feet, Doug stabs him with his stick and cuts him. Oh, he cuts him bad. It's an 18-stitch job. He goes off the ice and he's bleeding like a war hero. That puts an end to any more of the fans coming on the ice ...," said Storey.

The Canadiens went on to win their fourth consecutive Stanley Cup. Harvey's streak of winning the Norris Trophy was broken at four years in 1959, but he would win it the following year and two years after that, for seven in all. The Habs won their record-breaking fifth consecutive Stanley Cup in 1960. But changes were afoot.

The Canadiens could no longer count on their unrivalled supremacy to carry them through a season. The Chicago Blackhawks, led by the blond-haired dynamo Bobby Hull, were supplanting Montreal as the most exciting and offensively potent team in the league. And the Maple Leafs under Punch Imlach were becoming a force to be reckoned with.

Within the Canadiens' dressing room, a living legend was about to call it a career. When Maurice Richard retired after the first day of training camp in 1960, Doug Harvey was elected to replace him as captain. Many had wanted Harvey to be captain when Butch Bouchard retired six years earlier, but Canadiens' management, upset over his hard-living lifestyle and anti-authoritarian views, nixed the move.

Canadiens' manager, Frank Selke, had been looking for any excuse to get rid of Harvey. If it were up to him, Selke would have banished Harvey from Montreal the moment he and Ted Lindsay announced they were putting together the players' association back in 1957. Team ownership overruled Selke. Winning Stanley Cups was more important than winning a labour–management battle, and the Canadiens were winning Stanley Cups. It also would have taken a public relations sleight of hand to convince the loyal Canadiens' fans that trading the best defenceman in the league was beneficial.

But the Canadiens didn't win a sixth-consecutive Cup in 1961. Even though they had the best record in the league, they bowed out in the semi-finals to Chicago.

Selke publicly cast a great deal of the blame on his captain, even though Harvey again won the Norris Trophy. Harvey was traded to the New York Rangers. Manager Muzz Patrick was looking for a new coach and someone with veteran presence and a winning attitude to shore up his blueline. Harvey would be the Rangers' captain and coach. He would be paid $27,000 per season, one of the highest salaries in the league.

The Rangers were perennial NHL bottom feeders and had only made it to the playoffs three out of the previous 10 years. They hadn't won the Stanley Cup since 1940.

Harvey paid instant dividends, helping New York secure the fourth and final playoff spot, ahead of Detroit and Boston. He was able to bring the best out of players such as goaltender Gump Worsley, defenceman Harry Howell, and future superstar forward Andy Bathgate. He made the Rangers a more dangerous team. A number of times, he almost single-handedly brought the team from behind in a game, using the killer instinct honed by years of playing for the Canadiens.

The Rangers made the playoffs and lost gamely in the semi-finals. Throughout the season, Harvey had grown less and less fond of his role as coach. He missed being pals with the other players and hated being in a position of authority. Harvey disliked having to criticize the same players he would have to suit up with in the dressing room.

At the end of the season, despite persistent pleadings from the Rangers' management team, Harvey decided to give up the dual role and simply be a defenceman.

But 1962–1963 was a difficult season. Personal problems off the ice weighed on Harvey and affected his game. The denizens of Madison Square Garden began to boo him, and his bosses questioned their decision to make him the highest paid player in the NHL.

Although he rebounded somewhat in the second half of the season, the Rangers missed the playoffs again. Because Harvey had spurned the team's offer to be head coach, and to later become part of the front office, there was no longer a pressing need to keep him around.

Doug Harvey started the 1963–1964 season in the minors and was not in shape when brought up for a short stint with the Rangers. He was demoted, permanently, to Baltimore of the American Hockey League, but he decided to seek a release from his contract, and try the market as a free agent.

After bouncing around the minor leagues, Harvey still wanted to play the game at the highest level. At one point, he told the Rangers he would play for their farm team for free, just to prove he still had the goods. Detroit gave him a shot at the end of the 1966–1967 campaign, but the following year he was back in the bus leagues in Kansas City as the playing coach of the top farm team of the new St. Louis Blues.

The Blues, who were coached by Scotty Bowman and managed by Lynn Patrick, received reports all season about how well Harvey was working with the younger players and what a steadying influence he was in the dressing room. Although his stats were not particularly impressive, he could at times still control a game like the old days.

The Blues were in tough against the Philadelphia Flyers; the series was tied three games apiece. Bowman brought up Harvey to join fellow greybeards Dickie Moore and Glenn Hall, in time for the decisive game against the Flyers. The three battle-worn veterans led the young Blues to a 3-1 win. Moore assisted on the first Blues' goal, Harvey on the game winner, and Hall was brilliant between the pipes.

The next series against Minnesota also went seven games. At one point, the North Stars had a 1-0 lead late in the third period of the clinching contest. Many watching the game figured the Blues were done, and it would be the last time any of them would see Dickie Moore and Doug Harvey on the ice again.

At the end of regulation time, the score was 1-1. The tying goal had come from Moore, on an assist from Harvey. The Blues won the game and the series in double overtime.

The next series also went seven games, and Harvey's cool confidence helped keep his teammates' emotions in check. Bowman even credited him for talking a jittery Hall into playing the final game, when the always-nervous netminder said he couldn't.

The Canadiens swept the Blues in the finals, but every game was close. Even jaded Montreal reporters had to give Harvey, Moore, and Hall their due — they still had enough gas in the tank to make the Blues competitive. Harvey played in a remarkable 70 games in 1968–1969, but was injured late in the season, missing a second chance to play in the finals against the Habs. Montreal swept the Blues again, and the games were not as close.

By then even Harvey realized he had overstayed his welcome as an NHL player. He tried coaching in the Quebec Major Junior League but gave it up after a year. Already struggling with alcohol addiction, Harvey had difficulty adjusting to life as a normal person, no longer a star professional athlete. To the day he died, he believed his involvement in the players' association and his penchant for booze kept him from being elected to the Hockey Hall of Fame on the first opportunity. He was elected the next year, 1973, but declined to attend.

One of the last significant acts of his hockey-related life was advising Bill Dineen of the WHA's Houston Aeros to sign teenagers Mark and Marty Howe to contracts. The idea appealed to their dad Gordie so much that he came out of retirement to make it a Howe triumvirate.

Many saw Harvey as a tragic figure in his final years. Alcohol abuse had taken its toll on his health, and he was never able to maintain steady employment, although he never complained and never asked for handouts.

Toward the end of his life, he was voted to the Canadiens' all-time Dream Team, and even put on the Habs' payroll as a part-time scout.

He died a few days after his 65th birthday in December 1989. After his death, the man who covered most of his career, hockey writer Red Fisher, summed up Harvey's legacy best.

"[Harvey] always lived on the edge, whether it was waiting until the last possible split second to make a winning pass, or holding out on signing a contract until the last day of training camp. He was stubborn, aggravating, unselfish, hard drinking, fun loving — and the best defenceman, by far, in Canadiens' history."

Chapter 6
Allan Stanley:
Booed as a Ranger,
Beloved as a Leaf

t could be argued that Allan Stanley had two distinctly different professional hockey careers: the disappointing time spent in New York being booed mercilessly by dissatisfied and somewhat thick-headed Rangers fans who didn't understand a solid hockey player when they saw one, and the lengthy tenure as a member of the Toronto Maple Leafs, which included a number of All-Star Team selections and four Stanley Cup victories.

Stanley was deemed to be washed up by no fewer than three of the NHL's six franchises before the age of 33, and then went on to draw great praise in the second half of a 20-year pro hockey career. Allan Stanley was an amazing player, one who can be held up as an example of how persistence and perseverance pay off.

Stanley grew up in a part of northern Ontario that was a veritable breeding ground of hockey players. Before Shania Twain reintroduced the world to the community, Timmins was known for two things: mines that produced gold, and hockey rinks that produced NHL players. Allan Stanley, Real Chevrefils, Bep Guidolin, and Bill Barilko all hailed from Timmins, and dozens of others over the years have come from the surrounding villages.

The mines brought jobs, and jobs begat communities. In hard-working towns like Timmins, sports was a major factor in everyday life — a form of recreation and entertainment for residents.

Wealthy mine owners often sponsored sports teams, and, in some cases, entire leagues. Mines paid for arenas and ball diamonds to be built, so their employees had a healthy form of recreation, and their kids a place to play.

The competitive nature of mine owners also led to a lot of wagering, so owners would bring in top players from other parts of the country, give them a job in the mines, and put them on their hockey teams.

There was no minor hockey organization as we know it today, in the Timmins of Stanley's youth. There were plenty of outdoor rinks and frozen ponds on which to play shinny, but no league structures, which suited most of the kids just fine.

A local businessman who wanted to create a juvenile

team to play against other mining communities brought together Stanley and a few of the other good local players. Thus, the Holman Pluggers were born. For the first couple of years, the Pluggers played any other willing team. Soon they entered a proper juvenile loop. There was little expectation that this talented, but somewhat rag-tag, bunch of players from Timmins would ever be successful. But, anchored by Stanley, and featuring a few players who would eventually be successful in the pro ranks, the Holman Pluggers soon became a bona fide *cause célèbre* throughout northern Ontario.

"In 1941–1942, we won our area, and then we played Kirkland Lake. Kirkland Lake beat us and I think Ted Lindsay was on that team. The following year, we won the all-Ontario Championship. We first won the north, and then we went over to Sudbury and beat Copper Cliff. And then we went down to Toronto and played a sudden death game in Maple Leaf Gardens against St. Catharines for the championship of Ontario in 1943, and we beat them 6-5," recalls Stanley.

This was a great shock to the southern Ontario hockey establishment. Although the scouts of the NHL teams were searching throughout Canada for prospective hockey talent, northeastern Ontario was still unbroken soil, waiting to be tilled. The Holman Pluggers, led by their tall, muscular 16-year-old defenceman Allan Stanley, made the scouts sit up and take notice.

One of the scouts was Baldy Cotton. A former star player

in the NHL, Cotton was now working as a talent scout for the Boston Bruins. Several players from the Pluggers, including Stanley, were invited to Boston's training camp. Others were invited to the camps of the Maple Leafs and Red Wings.

Stanley was impressive enough to warrant a contract offer to play as a 17 year old for the semi-professional Boston Olympics of the Eastern Amateur Hockey League (EAHL). He began to put up noteworthy numbers for the Olympics, including 42 points in 40 games in 1943–1944, earning all-star recognition while helping his team with the United States Amateur Hockey Championship.

Stanley was a budding star, and management of the Boston organization was watching. One night, the top brass came to see Stanley and the Olympics play; they wanted to see first-hand how good he was. They showed up unannounced at a game when Stanley was ill with a virus and played the worst game of his young career. Figuring that all the talk was just hype, they didn't sign him to a professional contract; instead he was "loaned" to the Providence Reds of the AHL.

In truth, he was sole property of the Reds, but was being closely watched by another NHL team, the New York Rangers, in case he panned out.

Stanley became more than a top prospect — he became a star. In the 1947–1948 season with the Reds, Stanley earned 41 points. Not only was he a constant offensive threat, but he was also gaining a reputation as one of the hardest blueliners to get around. He had great positioning, excellent wheels, and a fearsome bodycheck that made more delicate forwards think twice about venturing up his side of the ice.

The Rangers were impressed and wanted to add Stanley to their roster as soon as possible. They were not doing well in the standings or at the box office. They needed a stud on defence to help cut down the goals against, but also to draw fans to Madison Square Garden.

Because Providence was an independent hockey organization not affiliated with an NHL club, the Rangers had to deal with the Reds as an equal, even though the team was in a lower league.

The Rangers picked up Stanley in exchange for players Eddie Kullman, Elwyn Morris, and a number of minor leaguers, plus cash. The value of the trade was estimated to be around $70,000.

For fans making about one tenth the amount of money Stanley was traded for, expectations of brilliance were natural. It didn't help that Rangers' president, Frank Boucher, told reporters that he expected Stanley would be "one of the greatest players in the National Hockey League," adding that the trade was the biggest deal in the team's history.

Allan Stanley was under the microscope of New York fans from the moment he played his first shift in his first game in 1948 for the Broadway Blueshirts. He soon learned that the players in the NHL were a different breed from those in the EAHL or the AHL. In a game against the Detroit Red Wings, Stanley went into the corner with a Red Wing by the name of James Enio to dig for the puck.

"We collided with each other and fell together. Guess I must have fallen on top of him because when I started to get up, I braced myself on Enio's chest with my arm. Believe it or not, the next thing I knew was that he'd bit me. I'd never been bitten before in a hockey game," Stanley told the *New York Herald Tribune* in January 1949.

Angry at the attempt at cannibalism, Stanley tried to bash Enio into the boards, but Enio saw him coming and got his elbow up at the last minute. Now Stanley had a sore jaw — and a penalty, because Enio didn't have the puck at the time Stanley checked him.

"It just goes to show you. If you lose your head for a second in this game, it gets you into trouble," he said at the time.

Every move Stanley made on the ice continued to be scrutinized. Every missed pass or giveaway was magnified. He seemed at times to be slow and tentative. He wasn't making end-to-end rushes; he wasn't single-handedly winning games. It didn't take long for the boos to start billowing down from the rafters.

Stanley picked up 10 points in 40 games that season, but the Rangers won only 18 of 60 games to finish in last place in the six-team league. The team wasn't doing any better than they had before they picked up Stanley.

The boo birds were still there in Stanley's sophomore year, but the Rangers pulled it together and made the playoffs, edging Boston for the fourth and final playoff spot by seven points. Early in the playoffs, Stanley stepped up his play, as did goaltender Chuck Rayner, and sent the Canadiens onto the golf course.

"We were inspired. We got hot and we beat Montreal," said Stanley, years later.

In the finals, New York faced a tough Red Wings team that was missing star Gordie Howe. Still, no one figured the Rangers had a chance. But Stanley, showing poise beyond his 23 years, played brilliantly. The Rangers pushed the powerful Wings all the way to overtime in the seventh and deciding game of the series.

"We had them on the ropes. We had them 2-0. I got a penalty and they scored two goals, because in those days, you stayed in the box the full two minutes no matter how many goals they scored. But then we went ahead 3-2, and they tied it 3-3. Then we went ahead 4-3, and they tied it 4-4," he said.

In overtime, fellow Timmins native Pete Babando broke the heart of Stanley and the rest of the Rangers by beating Rayner to giver Detroit a 5-4 win and the Stanley Cup. The penalty that cost his team two goals was added to the list of apparent offences Stanley committed in the eyes of his critics.

The Rangers seemingly were never going to be able to repeat the performance of 1950, and Stanley bore the brunt of the fans' outrage. The Rangers didn't make the playoffs the next three seasons, bottoming out with another last-place result in 1952–1953.

Lynn Patrick, who was coaching the Rangers at the time, later remarked that Stanley was one of the key contributors in their run to the 1950 finals, and was shocked when he wasn't named to a post-season All-Star Team.

From the moment he first pulled on a Rangers jersey, fans expected Stanley to lead them immediately to hockey's promised land. Even members of the worldly and often jaded New York media were puzzled by the way fans harangued Stanley, four years after he had come to the team.

"Now it appears that because Stanley is big enough to play like [former Ranger bruiser] Ching Johnson did, the customers want him to belt onrushing forwards hard enough to send them hurtling into at least the fourth row of the side arena," wrote one New York columnist in January 1953.

Somebody should have told Allan Stanley ahead of time that New York hockey fans wanted someone who would put on a show, not just someone who did his job. He couldn't seem to convince New York fans that he was a good player. Some scribes practically pleaded with their readers to give the affable Stanley a break, pointing out just how effectively he had been playing.

Although a consummate professional, Stanley admitted that the catcalls and poor reception he received in his home arena wore on him, gave him sleepless nights, and affected-his play. Many defencemen set up behind their own goal and wait for their forwards to get moving before starting a break-out play. Stanley said he would try to limit the number of times he did that because behind the net was where the verbal abuse and taunting were most acute. Finally, at the end of his tenure with the Rangers, team management decided that Stanley would only play road games, thereby limiting the negative impact of the fans' hatred.

Ten games into the 1953–1954 season, he was sent from the eastern seaboard to the west coast of Canada, to finish out the season with the Vancouver Canucks of the Western Hockey League. In the less-stressful environment, Stanley returned to form, notching 36 points in 47 games, and was named a league All-Star.

He was brought back to the Big Apple the following season, but mainly to showcase him to be traded. The Chicago Blackhawks, who battled with the Rangers for last place each season, decided to revamp their lineup, and traded veteran defenceman Bill Gadsby for Stanley.

Over the 52 games he played for Chicago that 1954–1955 campaign, Stanley was an offensive dynamo, scoring 10 goals and adding 15 assists. But he appeared listless and ineffective the following year. Soon the Blackhawks would be the second team to give up on Stanley, dealing him for next to nothing to the team that first noticed him as a member of the Holman Pluggers 13 years earlier — the Boston Bruins.

Lynn Patrick, Stanley's former coach in New York, managed Boston. He figured Stanley wasn't being used properly, and that there was still a lot of untapped talent and effort in the lanky defender. But when the team's fortunes failed to improve, Stanley was traded to the Toronto Maple Leafs.

Coach Punch Imlach knew Allan Stanley could be a key cog in the championship machine he was building in Toronto. The rest of the league thought Imlach was crazy, but then they also thought he was crazy when he pushed for the acquisition of 13-year AHL goaltender Johnny Bower, who went on to become one of the greatest goalies in NHL history.

It was with Toronto that Stanley's second hockey career began. He flourished under Imlach. A strict disciplinarian, Imlach recognized talent and knew how to squeeze the most out of it.

Not long after his arrival at Maple Leaf Gardens, Stanley was paired up with another bruising northern Ontario defender, Tim Horton. Imlach had worked his magic, and the two became the most potent pairing in the league.

"We seemed to be natural together. We played as a pair. We seemed to know where each other was and what they were going to do and everything," Stanley said.

The Leafs became a powerhouse in the 1960s, and Stanley had a new lease on life. He had found his niche. Always regarded as a top offensive defenceman, Stanley became a stay-at-home rearguard, letting Horton handle most of the offensive forays.

Horton said he became a more confident player because

of Stanley. He knew that no matter what he did, Stanley would be there to back him up. If he rushed up the ice, Stanley would hold down the fort in the Maple Leafs' end. If he happened to mess up and let the puck or an opposing player get by him, Stanley was there to pick up the slack.

The two gelled on and off the ice, becoming close friends. Throughout the 1960s, Imlach would have the Horton–Stanley duo on the ice for all the important defensive zone face-offs and at the end of all close games.

When the Maple Leafs won three consecutive Stanley Cups from 1962 to 1964, much of the credit was given to the goaltending of Johnny Bower, along with the defensive play of Horton and Stanley.

Stanley became known for his steadiness and was praised by his coach and teammates for his overall excellence. Although Stanley didn't make the highlight reels in the second half of his career, his entire tenure with the Leafs could be considered a highlight. He was named to the NHL's Second All-Star Team in 1960, 1961, and 1966 — at age 40.

"Stanley was the best left defenceman in the business …," Imlach said in April 1966, a few days after Stanley's season came to an end when he suffered a devastating knee injury.

"Nobody can be called indispensable in a team game," Horton said at the time. "But if there was one guy we couldn't afford to lose, it was Stanley."

Considering his age and the knee injury, the press pre-

Allan Stanley

dicted that Stanley had played his last game. Not so. He was back in the blue and white beside his pal Tim Horton when the 1966–1967 season began.

Through an up and down year, one that saw players move in and out of the lineup with various injuries and ailments, no one expected much from the Over-the-Hill-Gang, as they were dubbed by one press wag. But the Leafs expected a lot of themselves. As he had done for nearly 20 seasons, Stanley stepped up his game, helping to stem the tide of the Chicago attack in the first round — a six-game upset over the heavily favoured Hawks.

The finals against Montreal were a see-saw affair. In the sixth game, in Toronto, the Leafs held a slim one-goal lead with under a minute remaining in regulation time. The Habs had pulled their goalie in favour of an extra attacker. The face-off was going to be deep in the Maple Leaf's zone to the left of Terry Sawchuk.

Imlach tapped Stanley on the shoulder and told him to take the draw against Montreal's Jean Beliveau. For this key play, and this critical time, Imlach sent out an-all veteran fivesome: Stanley, Horton, Red Kelly, George Armstrong, and Bob Pulford. The old warriors came through, as Stanley won the draw and tied up Beliveau long enough for Kelly to get the puck out to Armstrong, who fired it into the empty net to seal the win.

The Toronto Maple Leafs had won the Stanley Cup. It would be Allan Stanley's fourth and last Cup, but his playing days in the NHL were far from over.

The next year, at the end of the first expansion season, Imlach left Stanley unprotected. The second-year Philadelphia Flyers picked up Stanley to add a sense of stability and a veteran presence to a young team. Through shrewd drafting and trading, the Flyers began to build a contender team by the early 1970s.

Stanley says the key to his longevity was simply hard work. The lessons he learned growing up in a mining town in northern Ontario had paid off for 20 NHL seasons. A four-time Stanley Cup champion, Allan Stanley was inducted into the Hockey Hall of Fame, alongside Frank Mahovlich and Johnny Bucyk, in 1981.

Chapter 7

Tim Horton: Strongman on the Blueline

At the best of times, the Chicago Stadium was an uncomfortable place for visiting teams to play. It was loud, and the crowd always seemed on the brink of turning the old barn into an insane asylum. If the Hawks ever got ahead of their opponents, the ferocity of the cheering increased. If they fell behind, it was even more fierce.

In the sixth game of the 1962 Stanley Cup final, the sights and sounds, the intensity and passion, and the sheer energy in the building defied description.

Chicago was the defending Cup champions after a 23-year drought was broken by a team that featured Bobby Hull and Stan Mikita up front, Glenn Hall in goal, and Pierre

Pilote directing traffic from the blueline. They had dethroned the five-time champs from Montreal, but found themselves facing the gritty, artistically challenged, but effective Toronto Maple Leafs.

The Leafs won the first two games at Maple Leaf Gardens, but in front of the Windy City faithful, the Hawks stormed back to even the series, allowing only one goal against in the two home dates. Then in the fifth game, Toronto blasted eight pucks past the normally stingy Glenn Hall for an 8-4 win. If the Hawks couldn't get it together in the next game, they'd be facing the bleak, heartbreaking prospect of elimination — in the Stadium.

Tim Horton had really come into his own that past season with the Leafs. Although a veteran with a decade of big-league service, Horton had become a genuine offensive threat in this playoff run. He had scored three goals, and heading into the third period, had amassed a dozen assists in as many games.

Defensively, Horton, along with blueline partner Allan Stanley, was effectively keeping Blackhawk Bobby Hull at bay.

The sixth game was rough. Players were hitting each other with everything they had. No quarter was given, and there were glorious scoring opportunities at either end of the rink.

Then it happened: a goal by Hull broke the tension. The home team was showered with acclaim and applause, along with debris of all sorts — programs, paper cups, and hats.

If the Hawks could have capitalized on that wave of emotional energy, they very likely would have run away with the game and set up a seventh game back in Toronto. But the Leafs were lucky: Chicago's momentum and energy died away, as more than 10 minutes elapsed while the mess on the ice was cleared away. After the arena staff finally completed their task, Bob Nevin of the Leafs scored to dampen the remaining enthusiasm in the Stadium.

With the score tied, howls of disgust emanated from the crowd when the referee called Chicago's Eric Nesterenko for tripping at the 13:27 mark of the third period. Another break for the Maple Leafs.

While Chicago was short handed, the puck was fired back down towards goalie Don Simmons. Horton grabbed the puck, striding up the ice with a purposefulness that seemed to indicate something significant was about to happen.

As he raced up the ice, he dished the puck off to captain George Armstrong, who fed it back to him; then Horton noticed teammate Dick Duff in the clear. A rushing defenceman was a bit of a novelty in the NHL in those days, but Horton was adept at picking his spots.

This was one of those spots. His pass was a bit ahead of Duff, because Horton knew exactly how fast his diminutive teammate was. And the Kirkland Lake native didn't disappoint. He took another couple of quick strides, grabbed the puck, and deposited it past Hall for the go-ahead goal.

Horton's play was the highlight of the game. It was also

the highlight of the playoffs, as his 16 points were not only the best on the team, but second only to the dynamic Mikita in the entire post-season. Horton could have just as easily have been the goat of the game, as he was whistled off for a tripping penalty with only 58 seconds on the clock. But mercifully, the Leafs killed off the penalty, and claimed the Stanley Cup — their first since 1951.

Miles Gilbert (Tim) Horton was born in the rugged town of Cochrane in northeastern Ontario in 1930. It was the beginning of the Great Depression, and even in the normally prosperous mining communities of the north, unemployment and economic desolation had taken a firm hold. Horton's father, Aaron Oakley "Oak" Horton, worked for the Canadian National Railway, but he had to scrimp and save to buy his six-year-old son a complete set of hockey equipment at Christmas.

A stellar junior career in the Sudbury-area community of Copper Cliff led to a scholarship with the prestigious St. Michael's College in Toronto. This was one of two main junior feeder teams for the Maple Leafs, the other being the Toronto Marlies.

Playing for St. Mike's in 1947–1948, Horton notched a respectable 13 points in all 32 games the team played. Showing a proclivity for pugilism, he also racked up 137 minutes in penalties, as many of the heavyweights in the league decided to try their luck with the brawny young man.

In his second season at St. Mike's, Horton scored 9 goals

and 18 assists for 27 points, an impressive total for a defence-man in any league at the time. He was offered a chance to turn pro with the Leafs' primary farm club in Pittsburgh for the 1949–1950 season. That year, Horton was also called up for a game with Toronto. He played a scant few shifts, earning one minor penalty.

Horton apprenticed for two full seasons in Pittsburgh, where his ability to dominate a game was well established, before joining the roster of the Maple Leafs for good in 1952.

The Maple Leafs were not a good team for most of the 1950s. They couldn't seem to regain the magic they had when the team dominated the league in the late 1940s. However, some promising young players were coming down the pike, Horton being one of them. In his second full season, fans in Toronto got a taste of the offensive ability of the young bull, when he garnered 31 points.

Things didn't fare as well in the 1954–1955 campaign, when Horton suffered an injury that many figured would end his fledgling NHL career. On March 12, the Leafs were play-ing the New York Rangers at home in Maple Leaf Gardens. Horton, grabbing the puck from deep in his own zone, saw that he had an open lane. Legs pumping like pistons, Horton charged up centre ice towards the Rangers' end. New York defender Bill Gadsby was skating backwards toward his goal-ie, when he suddenly stopped. Horton, who had momentarily looked back down at the puck, didn't realize that Gadsby had stopped dead in his tracks. Horton skated into him — hard.

Poor ice conditions in the Gardens contributed to the injury. One of Horton's skates got caught in a rut, and remained planted, while the rest of his body fell backwards, snapping his leg. He had taken part of the hit with his jaw as well, and was knocked out.

"His leg was fractured in two places, and his jaw and cheekbone were broken. They had to pull one of his teeth and wire his jaw shut. He was in hospital for about six weeks and it looked like he'd never play again," teammate Bob Baun wrote in his memoirs.

Horton put his nose to the grindstone and rehabbed his injured leg like a man possessed. He returned for the final three-dozen games of the 1955–1956 season and allayed any fears of being brittle, making up for lost time by hammering opponents with frightening regularity.

Horton was rebuilding his solid NHL career when Punch Imlach joined the Maple Leafs before the start of the 1958–1959 season. Horton was now a seasoned veteran with a reputation as a solid, dependable player. He flourished under Imlach's administration.

After gaining control of the player personnel decisions with the Leafs, Imlach began to make moves. He rescued Johnny Bower from seemingly permanent exile in the AHL. He also saw that Horton needed someone steady to work with.

He had Carl Brewer and Bob Baun, but they were of a different generation, and they showed great potential as a duo themselves. Imlach heard that Allan Stanley was available from the Boston Bruins and snapped him up. A former captain of the New York Rangers, Stanley was a defensively responsible blueliner who knew his position and played it with quiet, simple efficiency. After trying him briefly with Baun, Imlach decided that Stanley would be a better counterpoint to the swift-skating, more offensively adventurous Horton.

Horton would be the yin to Stanley's yang, adding the speed and offensive punch that every good blueline combination needed. His legendary strength, coupled with the tall, lanky Stanley's wingspan of an albatross, made life difficult for opposing forwards trying to break through into the Maple Leaf zone.

Stories of Horton's strength are legion. Opponents and teammates alike speak about it with a sense of genuine awe, recognizing that Horton could have used it to do real damage to an opponent if he so chose.

"He wasn't a fist-fighter at all, but he was tremendously strong," said former teammate and coach Red Kelly. "He had strength and when he got ahold of somebody, that was it."

Larry Hillman tangled with Horton a couple of times when they were opponents, and then played with the fellow northern Ontario native with both the Maple Leafs and Buffalo Sabres. He said Horton acted as though he were afraid of what might happen if he unleashed his full strength on an opponent, so he resorted to using the bear hug. "He

Number 7 Tim Horton

very seldom fought. If somebody wanted to act up, he would just put the bear hug on them, and where're you gonna go?"

When Darryl Sittler was a rookie with the Maple Leafs, Horton was playing for the Rangers. In a game between the two teams, a brawl ensued, with all the players finding a dance partner wearing the colours of the opposition. Sittler was standing beside Horton, with his gloves off. When he was about to jump in to aid a teammate who was on the wrong end of a beating, Horton simply reached out his big mitt and grabbed the young player's arm. He only used his thumb and forefinger to hold onto Sittler's bicep, squeezing more and more tightly.

"The kind of thing your father might do when you were six or seven years old," Sittler said. "With about the same result; my arm went numb."

Horton quietly advised the rookie that it might not be in his best interest to join the kerfuffle. Sittler, no dummy even in his youth, agreed. "If Tim Horton had an Austrian accent, he would have been Arnold Schwarzenegger," Sittler said.

Stanley said that if you were a player on the losing end of a slugfest, you loved having Tim Horton on your team.

"A Leaf player would be on his back losing a fight, and Tim would rush in, lift the other guy off and throw him away, like he was tissue paper."

But there was more to Tim Horton than his strength and hockey ability. Off the ice, he was a kind, gentle man, who became mischievous when he had imbibed a few beverages of the adult variety.

Stanley said Horton was famous for trying to wake up Davey Keon late at night in his hotel room during training camp. One night in Quebec City, Stanley said it took eight or nine runs before Horton was able to bash through the heavy oak doors at the Chateau Frontenac.

Once through the door, Horton would overturn Keon's bed with Keon in it, then scurry back down the hall, cackling all the way.

"He just liked to be playful," said Larry Hillman, who played with Horton in both Toronto and Buffalo. "He'd have a few beers and just be full of piss and vinegar, and he might just like to cause a little havoc, nothing too drastic, just sort of fun things ...."

Imlach probably knew a lot of these shenanigans were going on, but let it slide during the exhibition season. He also cut his veterans some slack, particularly those who performed well.

That said, Imlach was still a traditionalist as far as the game went. He didn't really like it when his defencemen made unscripted, potentially dangerous offensive forays.

In one game during the 1960s, the Leafs were hosting the Chicago Blackhawks at Maple Leaf Gardens, and the Hawks were having a field day in the Toronto end of the rink. A couple of times, a Leaf defenceman found himself out of position, leading to a scoring chance for the visitors. This was dangerous with the likes of Bobby Hill, Kenny Wharram, and Stan Mikita.

A fire-breathing Imlach stormed into the dressing room and ordered all defencemen to hold their positions. "In no way should a defenceman make a rush up the ice. Get the puck to a forward as soon as possible, and let them take care of the scoring," he commanded.

Horton and Stanley were on the ice to start the second period, and on the very first play, Chicago came right at the two veterans. One of the Hawks tried to dipsy-doodle around the wily Stanley, who simply stopped the puck with his huge hoof and then began moving up the ice.

"I got down to the centre line and I could hear the ice crunching over to my right, and I knew one of our guys was coming," said Stanley. "And I just took a quick look to see who the heck it was, and here it was Tim. So now you had two defencemen having a rush against two of their defencemen," said Stanley, who also took a moment to see a flummoxed Imlach on the bench hollering up the ice in his direction.

Horton kept skating, breaking through a gap in the Hawk defensive pairing. At the same moment as he broke into the clear, Stanley flipped the puck in the air, over the defencemen and onto Horton's stick. Horton promptly went in and scored.

While he was upset, Imlach also trusted his key veterans and excused the disobedience. Some other players wouldn't have been so lucky, and would likely have received a razor-sharp tongue lashing, along with a ticket to the minors.

Horton was a key contributor on all four of the Stanley Cups the team won in the 1960s — 1962 through 1964, and the last hurrah in 1967. When expansion rolled around, the Leafs protected their experienced, veteran players; the expansion teams picked up their younger players, who may have contributed greatly in years to come.

This proved to be a foolhardy strategy, as the veterans' play deteriorated, plagued by injuries, while the few young players the team had were not yet ready for prime time. The

Maple Leaf ownership, in a crass cash grab, sold both of their major farm teams, so a number of their prospects were lost for good. The organization that Conn Smythe built — and the one that discovered and nurtured players like Horton — was systematically dismantled.

After the 1967 Cup win, Imlach coaxed Horton back for another season. Imlach was fired at the end of the 1968–1969 campaign, and Horton retired. Team executive, Harold Ballard, offered a huge raise — up to $90,000 — for Horton to return. After pondering the growing doughnut store chain that he was building, he decided that the money was just too good to pass up.

With the Leafs going nowhere in the 1969–1970 season, management decided to make some changes. Tim Horton, who had played nearly 1,200 games for Toronto, and had been with the organization since he came to St. Michael's College in 1947, was traded. He went to the New York Rangers in exchange for future considerations.

Some said that King Clancy, who had been a part of the Maple Leafs' organization as player, coach, manager, and sidekick since 1930, wept when he heard that Horton had been dealt to New York. It's not the sort of ending many would have expected for one of the most beloved of Maple Leafs.

The Rangers were a better team in the standings, and there were a couple of former Leaf teammates around to kibitz with, so Horton wasn't too unhappy. But the Rangers were no better or worse than before they had Horton, and decided to expose him in the intra-league draft at season's end. The Pittsburgh Penguins, now coached by Horton's former Leafmate Red Kelly, decided to pick up Horton to add some experience to a woeful Penguins blueline.

Horton only played 44 games with Pittsburgh, and was exposed again in the intra-league draft at the end of the 1971–1972 season, after announcing (again) his retirement. A familiar face jumped at the chance to grab him.

Punch Imlach had landed with the expansion Buffalo Sabres as their general manager before their inaugural season in 1970–1971. He managed to lure a number of veteran players to the team, but also drafted young players who would become the cornerstone of the franchise in years to come.

Times had changed. The swinging 1960s had become the hedonistic anti-authoritarian 1970s. Players had agents, grew their hair long, didn't respond to threats of demotion or other forms of punishment, and made a lot more money then those in the 1950s and 1960s. Players didn't have the same level of commitment to teams as in past years, so Imlach was worried that the partying of the younger players would lead to poor performances on the ice. He needed to bring in someone like Horton and another former Leaf blueliner, Larry Hillman, as steadying influences.

Horton's maturity and experience helped him stay unruffled in tough situations, or when the team was facing adversity. "Sure our kids ... were developing quickly, but adding Tim was the principal factor in giving us the mix we needed. At the end of the season the players themselves voted him the team's most valuable player — not bad for a man of 43," wrote Imlach in his memoirs.

The Sabres made the playoffs for the first time that season — Horton's first with the team. They drew the Montreal Canadiens in the opening round. Buffalo lost the first two games in Montreal, and the first game back in Buffalo. Coach Joe Crozier rallied the Sabres to a series-saving 3-1 win. They also won the next game, 3-2 in overtime, but dropped the sixth game 4-2, to lose the series. There was some consolation in that Montreal went on to win the Stanley Cup.

Horton vowed that the 1973 playoffs would be his last time donning blades in the NHL. Imlach spent a great deal of time haggling with Horton to convince him to return. Imlach offered him a substantial raise, but before Horton would sign the contract, he extracted a unique signing bonus. He said he wanted an Italian-made sports car called a Pantera.

Against his better judgment, and to his eternal chagrin, Imlach relented. "You know something? I'm dead against giving you this car. You're liable to kill yourself with the damn thing," Imlach said to Horton at one point. Horton signed, and Imlach had his blueline anchor back.

Even into his early 40s, Horton's strength was still something to be reckoned with. Back in his first season with the Sabres, Buffalo was tangling with the Broad Street Bullies themselves — the Philadelphia Flyers in one early-season encounter.

The biggest and baddest of the Bullies, Dave "The Hammer" Schultz, suddenly grabbed Horton and threw him to the ice, with the intention of pummeling him into submission. Horton grabbed the bigger, burlier Schultz around the waist, and rolled the bigger man over so that Horton was on top. Horton, at 44 years of age, proceeded to shake Schultz around like a rag doll. Horton also never threw a punch. Even then, in his anger, he realized the damage he might have done, and resisted the temptation to teach a painful lesson to The Hammer.

Tim Horton was the third star of the game on February 20, 1974, in Maple Leaf Gardens, even though he had taken an errant puck off his mountainous jaw at practice two days before. Those in attendance said he was the best player on the ice, despite intense pain that sidelined him for much of the third period.

Horton stayed after the game and chatted with the likes of Dave Keon and Ron Ellis before hopping into his car for the trip back to Buffalo. On the way, he stopped into the head office of his doughnut empire and had a couple of drinks. Whether it was the combination of the painkillers and the little bit of alcohol that may have dulled his reflexes, we'll never know.

What is known is that, travelling fast on the barren Queen Elizabeth Way through St. Catharines, the wheels of his Pantera momentarily touched the shoulder on a slight curve in the road. Horton lost control and the car flipped over several times. Not buckled in, Horton was thrown out through one of the gull-wing doors, and was crushed by the car. He died instantly.

Frank Mahovlich received a phone call in the middle of the night telling him the news of Horton's death. "I was stunned. I mean I was just stunned. I thought that Tim would never die. He was such a strong guy, I thought this guy was going to live to a 100 and something years old. We used to call him Superman because he was so strong. To hear that he died, I couldn't believe it, it was just amazing," he said recently.

Horton was elected to the Hockey Hall of Fame in 1977. While he never won the Norris Trophy as the best defenceman in the league, he was named to the NHL First All-Star Team three times plus three times to the Second Team. The last season he was named to the First All-Star Team was 1968–1969, when he was 39 years old. The other First All-Star defenceman that year was Bobby Orr, who was 20 years old. That one of the oldest players in the league was considered to be an equal of one of the youngest and certainly most dynamic players says something about the hockey player that was Tim Horton.

Acknowledgments

The author wishes to acknowledge all the great authors, journalists, and historians whose work not only inspired his own, but from which many of the quotes and information were drawn.

Brian McFarlane's *Original Six* series has provided quotes and anecdotes, as did his earlier work *Rare Jewel for a King*, a biography of the late, great King Clancy. William Brown's brilliant book on the history of the Montreal Maroons was sourced, as was his biography of Doug Harvey.

Due reverence must be paid to Stan Fischler for his books *Those Were the Days, The Flakes of Winter, Bobby Orr and The Big Bad Bruins, Slashing,* and his *Hockey Encyclopedia.*

Dick Irvin's two autobiographies, *Now Back to You Dick,* and the later *My 26 Stanley Cups*, were great sources of information on the Original Six era and Doug Harvey in particular.

Douglas Hunter's biography on Tim Horton is a must read, while his coffee-table book, *Champions,* provided information about the Ottawa Senators.

Frank Boucher's memoirs, *When the Rangers Were Young,* and Eric Whitehead's book on the Patricks helped tremendously in learning more about Ching Johnson.

My newspaper career and previous books also helped in

the writing of this book, as I was able to go back to old interviews and bring some of the unused material to light. Much
of the Tim Horton chapter came from previous interviews I
conducted with Frank Mahovlich, Red Kelly, Johnny Bower,
Ron Ellis, Allan Stanley, and Larry Hillman, and many of those
same interviews helped shape the Allan Stanley chapter.

From their extensive clipping file, the research crew
at the Hockey Hall of Fame also helped fill in some gaps
with information about Dit Clapper and Allan Stanley. The
resource centre at the Hockey Hall of Fame is as much fun as
the Hall exhibits themselves.

Further Reading

Batten, Jack. *The Leafs* (2nd edition). Toronto: Key Porter Books, 1999.

Leonetti, Mike. *Canadiens Legends: Montreal's Hockey Heroes.* Vancouver: Raincoast Books, 2003.

MacInnis, Craig, editor. *Remembering Tim Horton.* Toronto: Stoddart Publishing, 2000.

McFarlane, Brian. *The Story of the National Hockey League.* New York: Charles Scribner's Sons, 1973.

McKinley, Michael. *Hockey Hall of Fame Legends.* Toronto: Viking Books, 1993.

Roxborough, Henry. *The Stanley Cup Story.* Toronto: McGraw-Hill Ryerson Ltd., 1971.

About the Author

Jim Barber is a graduate of Trent University in Peterborough, and Toronto's Centennial College.

He has been working in the community newspaper industry as a writer and editor for 13 years, winning numerous awards for writing and page design. His career has taken him to his hometown of Newmarket, Port Colborne, Kirkland Lake, Oshawa, Peterborough, and Collingwood. He is currently the Arts, Lifestyles and Sports Editor for the *Barrie Advance*, a Metroland community newspaper serving the growing central Ontario city.

Jim has written three other books for the Amazing Stories imprint — *Toronto Maple Leafs: Stories of Canada's Legendary Team; Montreal Canadiens: Thrilling Stories from Canada's Famous Hockey Franchise,* and the newly released *Great Goaltenders: Stars of Hockey's Golden Age.* He is also the co-ordinating editor for the Amazing Stories hockey sub-series.

He resides near Collingwood, Ontario, with his wife, Sheri, and two stepsons, Robin and David. Jim is very glad that the NHL and its players got their collective act together before the beginning of the 2005–2006 hockey season.

Photo Credits

Cover: Graphic Artists/Hockey Hall of Fame; Graphic Artists/Hockey Hall of Fame: page 114; Hockey Hall of Fame: page 40; Imperial Oil–Turofsky/Hockey Hall of Fame: pages 27, 66, 83, 104.

OTHER AMAZING STORIES

These titles are available wherever you buy books. If you have trouble finding the book you want, call the Altitude order desk at **1-800-957-6888**, e-mail your request to: **orderdesk@altitudepublishing.com** or visit our Web site at **www.amazingstories.ca**

New AMAZING STORIES titles are published every month.